The Merrill Studies in
A Farewell to Arms

Compiled by

John Graham
University of Virginia

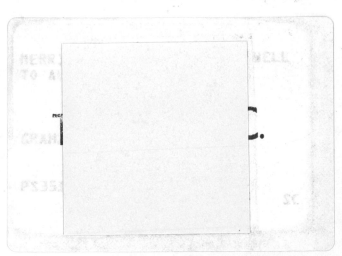

Charles E. Merrill Publishing Company

A Bell & Howell Company

Columbus, Ohio

CHARLES E. MERRILL STUDIES

Under the General Editorship of
Matthew J. Bruccoli and Joseph Katz

ISBN: 0-675-09231-0

Library of Congress Catalog Number: 75-143440

1 2 3 4 5 6 7 8 9 10—79 78 77 76 75 74 73 72 71

Printed in the United States of America

Preface

Remarque's *All Quiet on the Western Front* and Hemingway's *A Farewell to Arms* remain the most enduring novels of World War I. Remarque's novel is clearly and directly the story of the horrors of that war as lived by the men in the trenches. One of the major critical problems of *A Farewell to Arms* is that, although its perimeters seem rather carefully drawn, it is a combination of a story of love, of war, of a man, and of a woman. And if, in fact, this novel is a great one, all of the various stories must in some way interlock, must illuminate and complicate each other. I think no critic has yet described the rich interrelationships so the studies in this volume are but approaches to understanding and as a group constitute a question: where is the critic who will take this novel and write the full statement on it?

There is a second problem in the reading of *A Farewell to Arms*. A rather standard critical approach to any literary work is to read it, if not in the light of the author's other works, certainly seeking support from the author's entire body of writing. I believe that critics have been so preoccupied with the "Hemingway code" of the capable man stoically accepting the unreasonable demands of life that they have categorized all of Hemingway's major protagonists too neatly. By emphasizing the similarities rather than the differences the critics have interfered with the reading of any particular novel. The fact is Frederic Henry is not Jake Barnes nor is he Robert Jordan or Thomas Hudson.

In addition to the confusion by critics of the nature of the Hemingway characters, there is a further confusion, encouraged by Hemingway, of the author and his protagonists. Hemingway's work is significantly born of his experience: he drove an ambulance in Italy during World War I, was wounded, and loved a nurse, just as does Frederic Henry in *A Farewell to Arms.* But Ernest Hemingway is not Frederic Henry, and Frederic Henry is not Ernest Hemingway.

This novel of chaos, bone-weariness, and death needs to be read for itself to illuminate the experience of war, the experience of love, and the experience of art.

Further investigations of Hemingway's *A Farewell to Arms* should begin with *The Merrill Checklist of Ernest Hemingway,* compiled by William White (Columbus: Charles E. Merrill, 1970) and "Criticism of Ernest Hemingway: A Selected Checklist," by Maurice Beebe and John Feaster, *Modern Fiction Studies,* XIV (1968), 337-368, especially 354-356. Particularly handy items are anthologies of criticism by various hands: *Twentieth-Century Interpretations of "A Farewell to Arms",* edited by Jay Gellens (Englewood Cliffs, N.J.: Prentice-Hall, 1970); *Hemingway and His Critics: An International Anthology* (New York: Hill & Wang, 1961) and *Ernest Hemingway: Critiques of Four Major Novels* (New York: Scribner, 1962), both edited by Carlos Baker; *Ernest Hemingway: The Man and His Work* (Cleveland: World, 1950), edited by John K. M. McCaffery; *Hemingway: A Collection of Critical Essays* (Englewood Cliffs, N.J.: Prentice-Hall, 1962), edited by Robert P. Weeks; and *Studies in "The Sun Also Rises"* (Columbus: Charles E. Merrill, 1969), edited by William White.

Other significant studies are Ford Maddox Ford, "Introduction," *A Farewell to Arms* (New York, 1932); Edmund Wilson, "Hemingway: Gauge of Morale," *The Wound and the Bow* (New York, 1965, revised); Robert Penn Warren, "Hemingway," *The Kenyon Review,* IX (Winter, 1947), 1-28; William A. Glasser, *"A Farewell to Arms,"* *The Sewanee Review,* LXXIV, (Spring, 1966), 453-469; and William White, *The Merrill Guide to Ernest Hemingway* (Columbus: Charles E. Merrill, 1969). The review-articles in *Bookman,* LXX (November, 1929; February, 1930) reveal valuable contemporary views of the novel's "morality."

For continuing developments, see *Fitzgerald/Hemingway Annual,* 1969 (Washington: Microcard Editions, 1969). The definitive biography is Carlos Baker's *Ernest Hemingway: A Life Story* (New York: Scribner, 1969). A different and stimulating experience is to hear Hemingway reading his own works (Caedmon Records, TC 1185).

A number of the critics included in this gathering have used different editions of the novel. References can be easily found, however, since they fall very close to each other in any edition.

A few silent corrections have been made in the reviews and studies, mainly relative to the spelling of "Frederic" as "Frederick" and Catherine "Barkley" as "Barklay." But, in general, the critic's text is untouched even when English Catherine is referred to as Scotch.

Contents

1. Contemporary Reviews

monologues to his range of effects, and he has even begun to discuss ideas. In mood he reveals a new tenderness, and it is interesting to observe that the present volume is his first love story, properly speaking. It is also his first long story about the war, his first novel in the strict sense—"The Sun Also Rises" was an extended episode—and undoubtedly the most important book he has written.

"A Farewell to Arms" is perhaps the only American war novel in which the hero drives an ambulance. I find this somewhat remarkable, and for a very simple reason. Just as the typical British war novels are written by former captains of infantry, and German novels of the same class by privates with a just grievance, so the typical American war novels, beginning with "Three Soldiers" and perhaps not ending with the present volume, have been written by former ambulance drivers.

It is hard to say why this one branch of the army should have been so literary. Perhaps it is because young writers were patriotic in 1917, and because enlisting in the ambulance service was the quickest means of reaching the front. Perhaps it is because the idea of transporting the wounded, even in reconditioned Fords over bad roads, appealed to the romantic side of their natures. I doubt it. All I know for certain is that in one typical section of thirty men, there were three who later became professional writers, in addition to a painter, an architect, a philologist, and almost the whole football squad of a large preparatory school. The conditions were similar in other sections I visited; and, in fact, after reading a roster of the American Ambulance, one begins to regard it as a sort of college extension course for the present generation of writers.

But what did it teach? How did it color the minds of the young men who drove at the front? . . . The question is much too general. However, one important effect of the ambulance service on some of its members was to develop what might be called a *spectatorial* attitude toward the war.

. . . Sometimes, for three days at a time, troops came marching through the villages where we were quartered. Chasseurs slouching along in their dark blue uniforms; a regiment of Senegalese, huge men with blue-black faces and white teeth; a detachment of Moroccans; then a convoy of camions screeching along in first and second gears, keeping pace with the marching men. Behind them, hidden in dust, came an endless procession of seventy-fives with very blond artillerymen riding on the caissons, then a supply train, then two line regiments with their rolling kitchens, then wagons overloaded with bread. The Annamites, little mud-colored men with the faces of perverted children, watched from the ditches where they were breaking stone; the airplanes of three nations kept watch overhead; and we ourselves were watchers. It did not seem that we could ever be part of all this. We were drivers, not soldiers. This long parade of nations was a spectacle which it was our privilege to survey.

Once at sunset I remember halting in the courtyard of a roofless chateau. Shells were harmlessly rumbling overhead; the German and the French heavy batteries, six miles behind their respective lines, were shelling each other as if the war had been reduced to a private quarrel between them; here, two miles from the lines, it was as if we were lying underneath an elevated freight yard where heavy trains were being shunted back and forth. We listened absently and talked. We talked about Mallarmé—whom none of us would confess to not understanding—the Russian ballet and the respective virtues of two college magazines. On the steps of the chateau four boys from Andover were rolling dice. A dozen French batteries on the hillside were laying down a barrage; the guns flashed like fireflies among the trees, and farther to the north, over the lines, the first rockets were rising. We talked about Blake. We talked about the ambulance service, rather bitterly.

And yet, the ambulance service was almost ideal. Being attached to the French army, it freed us from the more severe American discipline. It provided us with fairly good food, a congenial occupation, furloughs to Paris and uniforms that admitted us to the best hotels; it introduced us to the vast spectacle of war; it confronted us with hardships, but not more of them than it was gratifying to endure, and with danger, but not excessive danger: seldom were there more than two or three serious casualties in a section during the year. And that was really the burden of our complaint. The war created a thirst for excitement in young men, and most of my friends were planning to have themselves transferred into branches of the army—of any army—that were richer in fatalities.

They scattered soon afterward; they joined the Lafayette Escadrille, the French or British field artillery, the Royal Air Force; the most romantic enlisted in the Foreign Legion and a few determined patriots in the American infantry. I had other acquaintances in distant sectors; one of them flew for the Belgians, another flew in Serbia, and several moved on to the Italian front, where Hemingway himself had driven an ambulance before enlisting for more arduous service with the Arditi. . . . Even in these new scenes, faced by new dangers that cost the lives of many, they retained their curious air of detachment, of merely looking on.

Meanwhile let us return to the novel and to Frederic Henry, American volunteer with the Italian army and lieutenant in charge of an ambulance section on the Isonzo front. His associates were less intellectual than those he might have met on the Chemin des Dames: most of them were tired and very middle-class Italian officers. However, his own attitude was the one I have tried to describe: that of a spectator who was beginning to lose his interest.

This attitude is especially evident in the first part of the novel. Everything—the war, the weather, the epidemic of cholera, the conversation at the mess table—is repeated impartially, as from a great distance or by the military observer of a neutral power. Even when the hero is wounded by a trench mortar he is only the spectator of his own disaster. "I sat up straight," he says, "and as I did so something inside my head moved like the weights on a doll's eyes and it hit me inside in back of my eyeballs. My legs felt warm and wet and my shoes were wet and warm inside. I knew that I was hit and leaned over and put my hand on my knee. My knee wasn't there. My hand went in and my knee was down on my shin. I wiped my hand on my shirt and another floating light came very slowly down and I looked at my leg and was very afraid."

He was carried off to the dressing station, still observing the war and his own wounds dispassionately. However, he was destined to be carried out of himself by two events which together form the plot of the novel. The first was his falling in love. The second was the Italian retreat from the Isonzo.

In Gorizia, before being wounded, he had met an English nurse and had desired her merely because "this was better than going every evening to the house for officers where the girls climbed all over you and put your cap on backward as a sign of affection between their trips upstairs." He met her again in Milan while in the hospital and fell completely and suddenly in love. She went on night duty to be alone with him. They would be married soon, very soon, the moment they could obtain the necessary papers. Catherine was going to have a child.

He was ordered back to the front before anything had really been arranged. Three days after his return the Germans broke through at Caporetto. . . . The description of the Italian retreat, with its sleeplessness, its hunger, its growing disorganization, its lines of tired men marching in the rain, is perhaps the finest single passage that Hemingway has written. It calls to mind a great description by another writer: I mean Stendhal's account of the retreat from Waterloo. The two are by no means equal, but it is enough that they can be mentioned in the same breath.

At the end of the long wooden bridge over the Tagliamento Henry was halted by the battle police. They had been executing every officer above the rank of captain for abandoning his troops; now they were about to execute this American because he spoke Italian with an accent and might possibly be a spy. He escaped from them by diving into the flooded river; he made his way to Milan; he followed Catherine to Lake Maggiore, and the two of them, now both deserters, crossed the Swiss frontier at night. The passage that follows is a long winter idyll, the life of two lovers alone in the mountains, a tender contrast to the retreat through the Venetian plain. The novel ends, however, in another hospital: it ends with Catherine dying in childbirth and with her lover standing beside her body after having ordered the nurses to leave the room. The final paragraph is entirely typical of Hemingway's method: it implies all the emotion of the scene by a simple statement of the acts performed:

> "But after I had got them out and shut the door and turned off the light it wasn't any good. It was like saying good-bye to a statue. After a while I went out and left the hospital and walked back to the hotel in the rain."

One cannot help thinking that "A Farewell to Arms" is a symbolic title: that it is Hemingway's farewell to a period, an attitude, and perhaps to a method also. . . . As the process of demobilization draws slowly to its end the simple standards of wartime are being forgotten. Pity, love, adventurousness, anger, the emotions on which his earlier books were based, almost to the entire exclusion of ideas, are less violently stimulated in a world at peace. The emotions as a whole are more colored by thought; perhaps they are weaker and certainly they are becoming more complicated. They seem to demand expression in a subtler and richer prose. The present novel shows a change in this direction, and perhaps the change may extend still farther—who knows. Perhaps even Hemingway may decide in the end that being deliberately unsophisticated is not the height of sophistication.

T. S. Matthews

"Nothing Ever Happens to the Brave"

The writings of Ernest Hemingway have very quickly put him in a prominent place among American writers, and his numerous admirers have looked forward with impatience and great expectations to his second novel. They should not be disappointed: "A Farewell to Arms" is worthy of their hopes and of its author's promise.

The book is cast in the form which Hemingway has apparently delimited for himself in the novel—a diary form. It is written in the first person, in that bare and unliterary style (unliterary except for echoes of Sherwood Anderson and Gertrude Stein), in that tone which suggests a roughly educated but sensitive poet who is prouder of his muscles than of his vocabulary, which we are now accustomed to associate with Hemingway's name. The conversation of the characters is as distinctly Hemingway conversation as the conversation of one of Shaw's plays is Shavian. But there are some marked differences between "A Farewell to Arms" and Hemingway's previous work.

Reprinted from *The New Republic,* LX (October 9, 1926), 208-210. Reprinted with permission.

For one thing, the design is more apparent, the material more solidly arranged. Perhaps the strongest criticism that could be levelled against "The Sun Also Rises" was that its action was concerned with flotsam in the eddy of a backwater. It was apparently possible for some readers to appreciate the masculinity of Hemingway's "anti-literary" style, to admit the authenticity of his characters, and still to say, "What of it?" This criticism I do not consider valid—there has always been, it seems to me, in the implications of Hemingway's prose, and in his characters themselves, a kind of symbolic content that gives the least of his stories a wider range than it seems to cover—but such a criticism was certainly possible. It is not, however, a criticism that can possibly be directed against "A Farewell to Arms." Fishing, drinking, and watching bullfights might be considered too superficial to be the stuff of tragedy, but love and death are no parochial themes.

. . . .

The book has more in it than "The Sun Also Rises"; it is more of a story; and it is more carefully written. Sometimes this care is too evident.

> I had gone to no such place but to the smoke of cafés and nights when the room whirled and you needed to look at the wall to make it stop, nights in bed, drunk, when you knew that that was all there was, and the strange excitement of waking and not knowing who it was with you, and the world all unreal in the dark and so exciting that you must resume again unknowing and not caring in the night, sure that this was all and all and all and not caring. Suddenly to care very much and to sleep to wake with it sometimes morning and all that had been there gone and everything sharp and hard and clear and sometimes a dispute about the cost.

This is a good description, but it is Hemingway gone temporarily Gertrude Stein. There is one other striking example of this manner, not new to Hemingway, but new to his serious vein:

> "I love your beard," Catherine said. "It's a great success. It looks so stiff and fierce and it's very soft and a great pleasure."

This speech of Catherine's occurs toward the end of the book. When she is first introduced, she talks, plausibly enough, in a manner which, though distinctly Hemingway, might also pass as British. In the last half of the book (except for the Gertrude Stein lapse quoted above), she is pure Hemingway. The change that comes over her, the change that comes over both the main characters, is not, I think, due to the author's carelessness. Whether he deliberately planned this metamorphosis or half-consciously allowed it to take place is of minor interest. The interesting and the significant thing is the nature of the change. A typical Hemingway hero and a not-quite-so-typical Hemingway heroine are transformed, long before the end, into the figures of two ideal lovers.

Hemingway has been generally regarded as one of the most representative spokesmen of a lost generation—a generation remarkable chiefly for its cynicism, its godlessness, and its complete lack of faith. He can still, I think, be regarded as a representative spokesman, but the strictures generally implied against his generation will soon, perhaps, have to be modified or further refined. As far as Hemingway himself is concerned, it can certainly no longer be said that his characters do not embody a very definite faith.

"They won't get us," I said. "Because you're too brave. Nothing ever happens to the brave."

Rinaldi, the Italian surgeon who is the hero's room-mate in the first part of the book, has what almost amounts to a breakdown because he can discover nothing in life outside his three anodynes of women, wine and work. The note of hopelessness that dominated the whole of "The Sun Also Rises" is not absent in "A Farewell to Arms," nor is it weaker, but it has been subtly modified, so that it is not the note of hopelessness we hear so much as the undertone of courage. Hemingway is now definitely on the side of the angels, fallen angels though they are. The principal monument of this change is Catherine. Brett, the heroine of "The Sun Also Rises," was really in a constant fever of despair; the selfless faith which Catherine gives her lover may seem to come from a knowledge very like despair, but it is not a fever. When we look back on the two women, it is much easier to believe in Brett's actual existence than in Catherine's—Brett was so imperfect, so unsatisfactory. And, like an old soldier, it would have been wrong for Brett to die. The Lady in the Green Hat died, but Brett must live. But Catherine is Brett—an ennobled, a purified Brett, who

can show us how to live, who must die before she forgets how to
show us—deified into that brave and lovely creature whom men,
if they have never found her, will always invent.

This apotheosis of bravery in the person of a woman is the
more striking because Hemingway is still the same apparently
blunt-minded writer of two-fisted words. He still has a horror of
expressing delicate or noble sentiments, except obliquely.

> I did not say anything. I was always embarrassed by the words
> sacred, glorious, and sacrifice and the expression in vain. We had
> heard them . . . and had read them, on proclamations that were
> slapped up by billposters over other proclamations, now for a long
> time, and I had seen nothing sacred, and the things that were
> glorious had no glory and the sacrifices were like the stockyards
> at Chicago if nothing was done with the meat except to bury it.
> There were many words that you could not stand to hear and
> finally only the names of places had dignity.

And his prophecy of individual fate is, if anything, more brutally
pessimistic than ever:

> The world breaks every one and afterward many are strong at the
> broken places. But those that will not break it kills. It kills the
> very good and the very gentle and the very brave impartially. If
> you are none of these you can be sure it will kill you too but there
> will be no special hurry.

He will not even call Catherine brave, except through the lips of
her lover. Here he is describing how she acted in the first stages of
labor:

> The pains came quite regularly, then slackened off. Catherine
> was very excited. When the pains were bad she called them good
> ones. When they started to fall off she was disappointed and
> ashamed.

Hemingway is not a realist. The billboards of the world, even as he
writes about them, fade into something else: in place of the world
to which we are accustomed, we see a land and a people of strong
outlines, of conventionalized shadow; the people speak in a clipped
and tacit language as stylized as their appearance. But Hemingway's report of reality is quite as valid as a realist's./The description of the War, in the first part of "A Farewell to Arms," is

perhaps as good a description of war just behind the front as has been written; and a fresh report from a point of view as original as Hemingway's is an addition to experience. But this book is not essentially a war-story; it is a love-story. If love-stories mean nothing to you, gentle or hard-boiled reader, this is not your book. /

The transition, indeed, from the comparative realism of the war scenes to the ideal reality of the idyll is not as effective as it might be. The meeting of the lovers after Henry's desertion from the army, and their escape into Switzerland, have not that ring of authenticity about them which from Hemingway we demand. We are accustomed to his apparent irrelevancies, which he knows how to use with such a strong and ironic effect, but the scene, for instance, between the lovers and Ferguson in the hotel at Stresa seems altogether too irrelevant, and has no ironic or dramatic value, but is merely an unwanted complication of the story. From this point until the time when the lovers are safely established in Switzerland, we feel a kind of uncertainty about everything that happens; we cannot quite believe in it. Why is it, then, that when our belief is reawakened, it grows with every page, until once more we are convinced, and passionately convinced, that we are hearing the truth?

I think it is because Hemingway, like every writer who has discovered in himself the secret of literature, has now invented the kind of ideal against which no man's heart is proof. In the conclusion of "A Farewell to Arms," he has transferred his action to a stage very far from realism, and to a plane which may be criticized as the dramatics of a sentimental dream. And it is a dream. Catherine Barkley is one of the impossibly beautiful characters of modern tragedy—the Tesses, the Alyoshas, the Myshkins—who could never have existed, who could not live even in our minds if it were not for our hearts. In that sentimentalism, that intimation of impossible immortality, poets and those who hear them are alike guilty.

Hemingway himself is doubtless a very different sort of man from the people pictured in his books; he may well have very different ideas about the real nature of life; but as long as books remain a communication between us, we must take them as we understand them and feel them to be. "Nothing ever happens to the brave." It is an ambiguous statement of belief, and its implications are sufficiently sinister, but its meaning is as clear and as simple as the faith it voices. It is a man's faith; and men have lived and died by much worse.

Henry Seidel Canby

A Review of *A Farewell to Arms*

When Mr. Hemingway dawned upon his native land with "The Sun Also Rises" he was received with mingled praise and doubt. His skill as a story-teller was evident, his dialogue was superb, he had that gift of creating a vivid reality which makes any suit trumps for a novelist, but his subject matter troubled the serious minded. So much art seemed wasted upon the lovable but futile revellers who ran from cocktail to cocktail up and down France, self-tortured, but flippant, as unmoral as monkeys yet pathetically appealing for sympathy in their mental woes (which were usually aggravated by a headache).

Since then we have had many short stories and this full-length novel, and now his scope and purpose become clearer. Those restless, witty youngsters of "The Sun Also Rises," charming even when drunk, were not trying to escape from life so much as from the anarchic whirl of their own minds. They were war neuroses, the electrons of a youthful generation dislodged by the rays of conflict and bombarding through the ether. Whether good physics

Reprinted from *The Saturday Review of Literature* (October 12, 1929), pp. 231-232. Reprinted by permission.

or not, the comparison is instructive, for an electron, never still, meaning nothing except as a symbol, never all at one place at one time, is an exact similitude of the nervous wanderers from bar to bar and *plage* to bull ring.

The physical disturbance has subsided since "The Sun Also Rises." In "Farewell to Arms," war is confessedly the disintegrant, but the hero has found meaning in existence again. While the futile Italian army beats in vain against the white Austrian peaks, and the war sickens, and there is no more sense in valor or loyalty and only kindliness and good humor left in the world; when the fugitives crowd down from Caparetto, and honest men are shot as traitors, and the best soldiers want only to go home; then the trifling amour between an American lieutenant in the Italian service and an English nurse, which is the opening theme of this novel, intensifies to a love which is something to grip the imagination and risk life for. Human particle uniting to human particle turns accident into substance again. And in place of the know-nothingness of his earlier philosophy, Hemingway gives us a youth who hates fate because it attacks "the very good and the very gentle and the very brave impartially/ If you are none of these you can be sure it will kill you too, but there will be no special hurry." He stands up against fate and defies it and makes of his love tragedy an experience to hold fast to in the midst of a general debacle. We have passed from the anarchic to the stoic view of things. Youth that stuck out its tongue at the world is playing the game. This is not reversal, it is only development.

/I do not think that this attempted philosophic analysis is taking Hemingway too seriously. You cannot take too seriously a novel of such vivid reality as "Farewell to Arms," nor an observer and auditor of such uncanny powers. Hundreds of writers have told the story . . . weariness of routine . . . a casual love affair . . . an obsession with loving . . . the subtle change from mistress to wife (Henry never actually marries Catherine, but that is irrelevant) . . . tragedy impending upon too much happiness . . . the poignant end. But it is not the plot that counts, it is the circumstances and the complete realization of the characters. In this book you get your own times in typical essence to wonder about and interpret. /

Yet I do not believe that Hemingway's strength lies in character creation. His Catherine and his Henry have nothing strange or novel in their personalities. Catherine is a fine girl who needs a lover. Henry is an individualist who acts by instinct rationalized not by principle, and makes his friends love him. Hemingway's art is to make such not unfamiliar characters articulate when he finds them. His minor people, like the pagan and affectionate Rinaldi, or old Count Greffi, playing billiards and discoursing wisdom at 94, are more original than his protagonists. It isn't *what* they are, it is *how* they are that seems important, and of course that is a true principle in art. Anyone can outline a psychology, but how many can give you, whole and self-interpreting, just a darky crossing the road, or a man nursing his first wound!

Hemingway works almost entirely through a simple record of incident and dialogue which he stretches to include meditation in the rhythm of thought. It is a fine art. He plays upon a principle which Robert Frost stated years ago, that every speaker has his own style and rhythm, unmistakable as his finger prints, and adds a discovery in which Gertrude Stein (who carries it into absurdity) helps him, that the recurrent rhythms of thought carry word repetitions with them, so that both dialogue and meditation can be charged with so much personality that further description is unnecessary.

"I'm going to have a baby, darling. It's almost three months along. You're not worried, are you? Please, please don't. You mustn't worry."

"All right."

"Is it all right?"

"Of course."

"I did everything. I took everything but it didn't make any difference."

"I'm not worried."

"I couldn't help it, darling, and I haven't worried about it. You mustn't worry or feel badly."

"I only worry about you."

"That's it. That's what you mustn't do. People have babies all the time. Everybody has babies. It's the natural thing."

"You're pretty wonderful."

"No I'm not. But you mustn't mind, darling. I'll try and not make trouble for you. I know I've made trouble now. But haven't I been a good girl until now? You never knew it, did you?"

"No."

"It will all be like that. You simply mustn't worry. I can see you're worrying. Stop it. Stop it right away. Wouldn't you like a drink, darling? I know a drink always makes you feel cheerful."

"No. I feel cheerful. And you're pretty wonderful." . . .

We were quiet awhile and did not talk. Catherine was sitting on the bed and I was looking at her but we did not touch each other. We were apart as when one comes into a room and people are self-conscious. She put out her hand and took mine.

"You aren't angry are you, darling?"

"No."

"And you don't feel trapped?"

"Maybe a little. But not by you."

"I didn't mean by me. You mustn't be stupid. I meant trapped at all."

"You always feel trapped biologically." She went away a long way without stirring or removing her hand.

" 'Always' isn't a pretty word."

"I'm sorry."

"It's all right. But you see I've never had a baby and I've never even loved any one. And I've tried to be the way you wanted and then you talk about 'always.' "

"I could cut off my tongue," I offered.

"Oh, darling!" she came back from wherever she had been. "You mustn't mind me." We were both together again and the self-consciousness was gone. "We really are the same one, and we mustn't misunderstand on purpose. . . . Because there's only us two and in the world there's all the rest of them. If anything comes between us we're gone and then they have us."

"They won't get us," I said. "Because you're too brave. Nothing ever happens to the brave. . . . You're brave."

"No," she said. "But I would like to be."

Nothing more is needed than just this for a story. Of course there are other ways. Dialogue can be conventionalized (like Elinor Wylie's) and then it is the ideas set in their own personal rhythm which give the effect of life. Or it can be made realistic as when taken out of a note-book record, and this, if the worst way, is sometimes effective. But Hemingway is after voice rhythms and voice contrasts. It is the way these people talk not what they say that lifts the scene into reality.

I see that he is being criticized for writing in English that teachers of writing would despair of because of its devastations of grammar and syntax. If the teachers despair, they are ignorant. Few experimenters are always successful, and when he does go really wrong, which is seldom, it is because in the attempt to make his English more expressive he overstrains an instrument which, at its best, is crude.

> Lying on the floor of the flat-car with the guns beside me under the canvas I was wet, cold and very hungry. . . . I could remember Catherine but I knew I would get crazy if I thought about her when I was not sure yet I would see her. . . . Hard as the floor of the car to lie not thinking only feeling, having been away too long, the clothes wet and the floor moving only a little each time and lonesome inside and alone with wet clothing and hard floor for a wife.

The rhythm of this last sentence is lovely, its success complete except just for an item of wilfulness which stopped him short in the last labor necessary to reconcile rhythm and sense.

> "I stay too long and talk too much." He was worried that he really did.

This is just sloppy English.

> Sometimes still pleasant and fond and warm and breakfast and lunch. Sometimes all niceness gone and glad to get out on the street but always another day starting and then another night and the difference between the night and the day and how the night was better unless the day was very clear and cold and I could not tell it; as I cannot tell it now.

This (in its context) is for all its looseness an admirable rendering of half articulate thought. Hemingway knows what he is about. Let his imitators beware lest they copy him, twisting syntax, not as he does to fit necessity, but out of bravado and freakishness. English is a great language, which makes rules for text-books, and its genius is to become more expressive not more correct.

I am sorry to have written so technically of such a human book, and yet cannot keep off this aspect where the author so loves his story that he makes a new style to get out all that he feels in it. It is not all style. There is a focussing of incident in the retreat from Caparetto, in the escape by night of the two on Lake Maggiore, and in the superb scene of childbirth that belongs to the great art of storytelling in general and would be admirable even if written in the straightforward method of the "Arabian Nights." But the vividness is from style.

"Farewell to Arms" is an erotic story, shocking to the cold, disturbing to the conventional who do not like to see mere impersonal amorousness lifted into a deep, fierce love, involving the best in both man and woman, without changing its dependence upon the senses, nor trafficking with social responsibility. It deals with life where the blood is running and the spirit active—that is enough for me. As for Hemingway's frankness of language, to object to it would be priggish. There is no decadence here, no overemphasis on the sexual as a philosophy. Rather, this book belongs with those studies of conjugal love which just now are interesting the French. If you set out to write of the love life of a man and his wife when that love life is central in their experience, why that love life is what you write about and frankness belongs to the theme.

A good Victorian, I think, would have admired the frankness of this book, and also its style, but might have felt it to be narrow to the point of triviality in its concentration. Our most skilful writers today are more interested in vivid snap shots than in cosmologies. They prefer carved peach stones to panoramas. I prefer either myself to the dull tales of "cases" so much admired a few years ago, in which fiction began to look like sociology. Hemingway does lack scope. He is attracted by the vivid, and doesn't care what is vivid so that he gets it right. It's a better way to begin than the opposite method of biographing the universe as one sees it and calling that a novel. Nevertheless, his eroticism will deserve a less specific name when he has learned how to do it (I think he has learned) and begins to use it as a factor in synthesis. Not that "Farewell to Arms" is a "youthful," an "experimental" novel. It is absolutely done; and, even cosmically speaking, the flow of great social resolutions down and away from battle in the Alps to disillusion in the plains until all that is left of emotion is canalized into the purely personal business of love— that is a big enough theme for any novel. It is only that his stories seem to lack experience beyond the baffled, the desperate, the indifferent, the defiant so far. Which means, I suppose, that he is wise not to have written in that penetrative way of his about what has not yet engaged the imagination of his generation. In fiction, he is worthy to be their leader.

Clifton P. Fadiman

A Review of *A Farewell to Arms*

Recently there have been laid down a number of dicta anent what the modern novel may not do if it is to remain a modern novel. One of them is to the effect that a representation of a simple love affair is impossible in our day. Another tells us that it is difficult, if not impossible, to reproduce the emotion of male friendship or love, as the present shift in sex conventions tends to surround the theme with an ambiguous atmosphere. A third dictum concerns itself with the impossibility of true tragedy in contemporary literature. A fourth, not so much a stated law as a pervasive feeling, would insist on the irrelevance to our time of the "non-intellectual" or "primitive" novel. Now, none of these generalizations is silly; there is a great deal of truth in all of them. It just happens that Mr. Hemingway, quite unconsciously, has produced a book which upsets all of them at once and so makes them seem more foolish than they really are. Worse still, his book is not merely a good book but a remarkably beautiful book; and it is not merely modern, but the very apotheosis of a kind of modern-

Reprinted from *The Nation,* CXXIX (October 30, 1929), 497-498. Reprinted with permission.

ism. Mr. Hemingway is simply one of those inconvenient novelists who won't take the trouble to learn the rules of the game. It is all very embarrassing.

Take the business of love, for example. Neither Catherine nor Henry in "A Farewell to Arms" is a very complicated person. They are pretty intelligent about themselves but they are not over self-conscious. There are few kinks in their natures. I don't suppose they could produce one mental perversion between them. They fall in love in a simple, healthy manner, make love passionately and movingly; and when Catherine dies the reader is quite well aware that he has passed through a major tragic experience. Their story seems too simple to be "modern"; yet it is as contemporary as you wish. It seems too simple to be interesting; yet it is gripping, almost heartbreaking. I don't think any complex explanations are in order. I offer the familiar one that Hemingway, almost alone among his generation, feels his material very deeply and that he never overworks that material. Understatement is not so much a method with him as an instinctive habit of mind. (It is more or less an accident that it also happens to harmonize with the contemporary anti-romantic tendency.) Consequently we believe in his love story.

Similarly with the second motif of the book: the emotion of male affection, exemplified in the relationship between Henry and Rinaldi. This is the most perilous theme of all. With some of us a fake Freudism has inclined our minds to the cynical. Others, simpler temperaments, inevitably think of comradeship in oozily sentimental terms, the Kipling strong-men-and-brothers-all business. Hemingway seems unaware of either attitude. Perhaps that unawareness partially explains his success. At any rate, without in any way straining our credulity he makes us feel that this very sense of comradeship—nordically reticent in Henry's case, blasphemously, ironically effusive in Rinaldi's—was one of the few things that mitigated the horror and stupidity of the war.

I have rarely read a more "non-intellectual" book than "A Farewell to Arms." This non-intellectuality is not connected with Hemingway's much-discussed objectivity. It is implicit in his temperament. He is that marvelous combination—a highly intelligent naif. I do not mean that he writes without thought, for as a matter of obvious fact he is one of the best craftsmen alive. But he feels his story entirely in emotional and narrative terms. He is almost directly opposed in temper, for example, to Sherwood Anderson, who would like to give the effect of naivete but can't because he is always thinking about his own simplicity. "A Farewell to Arms" revolves about two strong, simple feelings: love for a beautiful and noble woman, affection for one's comrades. When it is not concerned with these two feelings it is simply exciting narrative—the retreat from Caporetto, the nocturnal escape to Switzerland. The whole book exists on a plane of strong feeling or of thrilling human adventure. It is impossible to feel superior to Hemingway's primitiveness, his insensibility to "ideas," because he strikes no attitude. A large part of the novel deals with simple things—eating cheese, drinking wine, sleeping with women. But he does not try to make you feel that these activities are "elemental" or overly significant. They are just integral parts of a personality which is strong and whole. Therein lies their effect on us. It is impossible to be patronizing about Henry's, or Hemingway's, complete contemporaneity, his mental divorcement from the past, the antique, the classical, the gentlemanly, cultured tradition. "The frescoes were not bad," remarks the hero at one point. "Any frescoes were good when they started to peel and flake off." This is not merely humorous; it is the reflection of a mind reacting freshly, freely, with an irony that is modern, yet simple and unaffected.

"A Farewell to Arms" is not perfect by any means, nor, to me at least, interesting all the way through. I find the military descriptions dull, and for a paradoxical reason. Hemingway's crisp, curt, casual style, so admirably suited to the rest of his narrative, fails in the military portions because of these very qualities. It is too much like a regulation dispatch. Military reports have always been written in a sort of vulgar Hemingwayese; therefore they give no sense of novelty or surprise. But a detail like this does not matter much; the core of "A Farewell to Arms" remains untouched. It is certainly Hemingway's best book to date. There seems no reason why it should not secure the Pulitzer Prize for, despite the Italian setting, it is as American as Times Square. It is a real occasion for patriotic rejoicing.

B. E. Todd

A Review of *A Farewell to Arms*

There are two pictures, "The Soldier's Farewell" and "The Soldier's Return," reproductions of which may still be seen on the walls of inn-parlours. The first shows a young soldier saying good-bye to his relations, and the second his return as a wounded hero. They are both indicative of the glamour of war, and, though mildly pathetic, are in no way disturbing. There is, as a rule, a space on the wall between the two pictures—a space which seems to wait for a third one illustrating war. There is no such gap among our present-day word-pictures, as those who have read of the *quietness* of the Western Front will realize. And now, to assure us that there was no sweet hush on the Italian Front either, comes Mr. Hemingway's *A Farewell to Arms*. There is no glamour here, and few thrills: even the physical horrors described are not quite so ghastly as those in many war books. It is an epic of weariness.

The record of the young American who joined the Italian army is one of boredom, injustice, ineptitude, and waste. If more resent-

Reprinted from *The Spectator*, [England] CXLIII (November 16, 1929), 727. Reprinted with permission.

ment or fury were shown by the victims of chaos the book would be correspondingly more bearable. But there is little of that in this tale of weariness, so laconically written. Even the conversations are those of men, stupefied and numbed by boredom:—

> " 'Listen. There is nothing so bad as war. We in the auto-ambulances cannot even realize at all how bad it is. When people realize how bad it is they cannot do anything to stop it because they go crazy. There are some people who never realize.'
> 'I know it is bad, but we must finish it.'
> 'It doesn't finish. There is no finish to a war.' "

And so in the book there is no finish to the misery of the hero. When, after taking part in an authorized retreat, he is nearly shot for desertion, he abandons his arms and escapes into Switzerland, where he resumes a love-affair, begun at the front. All ends, as it began, in misery, and we are given a terrible glimpse of the horrors of birth worse than the previous ones of death by violence.

There may be cruder war books, but there are none gloomier than this very great one, which deserves a shelf of its own on that space on the wall, so that it can be used as an antidote to the sickly poison of glory and glamour.

2. Studies

Carlos Baker

Ernest Hemingway:
A Farewell to Arms

Since his death in the summer of 1961, a school of critics has arisen which holds that the novel we are about to discuss was really the last, rather than the second, of Hemingway's major works, and that his path as an artist from 1929 to 1959 was a gradual but steady descent. I do not hold with the opinions of this school, for it is my belief that though Hemingway's career as a writer was not without its ups and downs, he made as many triumphs in fiction during the last thirty years of his life as he had in the first thirty. This is not to say, however, that our critical brethren are necessarily wrong in preferring *A Farewell to Arms* over such later works as *For Whom the Bell Tolls* or *The Old Man and the Sea*. It is only to maintain that Hemingway continued to be a very able practitioner of the art of fiction for many years after the publication of *A Farewell*, and that we are not obliged to disparage the later work in order to admire the earlier.

Reprinted from Chapter 17 of *The American Novel from Cooper to Faulkner*, edited by Wallace Stegner, 192-205, © 1965 by Basic Books, Inc., Publishers, New York. Reprinted by permission of the author and the publisher.

Among the American novels which deal with the First World
War of 1914–18, *A Farewell to Arms* has stood up under the
weathering of the years as well as any and far better than most. A
number of his eminent contemporaries also wrote novels relating
to that war. To name only two for purposes of comparison, *Soldier's Pay* by William Faulkner and *Three Soldiers* by John Dos
Passos have long since begun to show signs of literary senility. No
reader who works his way consecutively through these three
novels could possibly doubt that the honors for continuing freshness, romantic derring-do, and simple reader-interest must be
awarded to Hemingway's book. It manages to remain singularly
undated at the same time that it perfectly embodies the *Zeitgeist*,
the governing moral essence of that far-away time.

Survival power in fiction may at first appear to be a most curious and chancy business. But perhaps it is not so curious, after all.
For Hemingway managed to catch and hold in his novel a set of
attitudes toward war and human love which are essentially ageless.
Moreover, the prose style in which he says his say about the people
he knew in that now-ancient war has remained for the most part
singularly invulnerable to the assaults of time. When he was
writing the book in 1928–29, he worked extremely hard, pruned
out excess verbiage with loving care, and rewrote extensively in a
considered attempt to fashion a kind of prose that would really
last. Malcolm Cowley once remarked that an astonishingly small
amount of Hemingway's prose has gone bad over the years. In the
same vein, Ford Madox Ford observed that Hemingway's words
strike us,

> each one, as if they were pebbles fetched fresh from a brook.
> They live and shine, each in its place. So one of his pages has
> the effect of a brook-bottom into which you look down through
> flowing water. The words form a tessellation, each in order beside
> the other. It is a very great quality. . . . The aim—the achieve-
> ment—of the great prose writer is to use words so that they shall
> seem new and alive because of their juxtaposition with other
> words. This gift Hemingway has supremely.[1]

Hemingway's posthumous reward for his long labors, which were
often carried on under conditions of extreme domestic duress, is
that we can still read with pleasure what was first set down in

---

[1] Ford, Introduction to *A Farewell to Arms* (New York: Modern Library,
1932), p. xvi.

typescript nearly forty years ago. Another part of our pleasure comes from his ability to give us that sense of vicarious participation in events long gone, which is one of the best reasons for reading that anyone has yet been able to discover. None of the histories of the war as it was fought on the Italian-Austrian front can possibly reproduce so exactly how it felt to be under fire, to hear the whump of descending shells during the horrendous bombardments, to carry the wounded to safety unless they hemorrhaged and died along the way, to share wine and rough talk with Italian officers in the regimental messrooms, or to experience the acute physical discomforts of rain and cold and mud and hunger and fear during an inglorious military retreat. Far better than factual history, fiction can seize and hold such experiences as these. Hemingway caught the accents and attitudes of that far-off time so exactly that they have stayed preserved for us in perfect condition, like the honeybee embalmed forever inside the burnished lump of amber.

The literary history of *A Farewell to Arms* is of more than common interest. Except for an accident, it might have been Hemingway's first novel rather than his second. As early as 1922, more than four years before the publication of *The Sun Also Rises*, he had begun to write a story about a young American ambulance driver on the Italian-Austrian front during the First World War. It seems to have been highly romantic in manner and conception. It was also written in a prose style considerably more elaborate and adjectival than the one we customarily associate with the young Hemingway. But this early version of the novel, such as it was, has been missing these forty years. The probabilities are that it long ago dissolved in the waters of a Parisian sewer or went up in flames to kindle someone's kitchen fire in the slums of the capital. For the valise in which it was being carried to Hemingway by his young wife was stolen by a petty thief in the Gare de Lyon in Paris one winter afternoon late in 1922. With it went the typescripts and longhand copies of several other early stories of Hemingway's—virtually all that he had written up to that time. Dismayed and disheartened by his loss, Hemingway did not again try to tell the Italian story until 1928, nearly ten years after the events on which the narrative is based had actually taken place.

Hemingway's own account of his second major attempt to write the novel is also rather dramatic, both geographically and domestically. Few books have been set down in such a variety of places. It was begun in Paris, and continued in Key West, Florida;

Piggott, Arkansas; Kansas City, Missouri; and Sheridan, Wyoming. He finished the first draft while living on a ranch near Big Horn, Wyoming. During this period, his second wife, Pauline, was delivered of a son by Caesarean section in Kansas City, and while he was revising his first draft, his father committed suicide by shooting himself in Oak Park, Illinois. Hemingway said:

> I remember all these things happening and all the places we lived in and the fine times and the bad times we had in that year. But much more vividly I remember living in the book and making up what happened in it every day. Making the country and the people and the things that happened, I was happier than I had ever been.

This creative happiness in constructing a narrative of doom bears a curious resemblance to an event which took place only a few years before Hemingway began to write. A visitor to Thomas Hardy's house near Dorchester in England was turned away firmly by the writer's wife. Mr. Hardy, she explained, was busily composing an extremely gloomy poem, and he was enjoying himself so much that he must not under any circumstances be disturbed.

The special pleasure that Hemingway took in his work arose no doubt from his recognition of how much better this fresh new version of the novel was turning out than the one he had lost to the petty Parisian thief a half-dozen years before. Now, with the experience of a first novel behind him, and with more than twenty-five published short stories to his credit, he was at last in a position to do justice to his romantic subject. For in the meantime he had grown up to his task.

He was also succeeding in following a piece of advice he had once offered to his friend and fellow novelist, F. Scott Fitzgerald. If something has hurt you badly, he argued, you must find a way to use it in your writing. You had better not moan and complain about past or present difficulties or personal misadventures. Instead you must use your misfortunes as materials for fiction. If you can write them out, get them stated, it is possible to rid yourself of the soreness in your soul. Although Hemingway on occasion spoke scornfully about William Wordsworth, there is a passage in the poet's great ode which precisely sums up Hemingway's position. "To me alone there came a thought of grief," said Wordsworth. "A timely utterance gave that thought relief, and I again am strong." Or, as Hemingway himself put it in a more modern idiom, "The fact that the book was a tragic one did not make me unhappy since I believed that life was a tragedy and knew it could only have one end." But the business of creativity was the great business. Now, in the late 1920's, setting down a romanticized fictional version of some of the things that had happened to him personally ten years before, Hemingway discovered in the process a greater pleasure than any he had previously known. "Beside it," he said, "nothing else mattered."

The pain and sorrow which he was now using in his novel were based on a double actuality: a pair of traumatic events from 1918–19, neither of which he had been able to forget, even had he wished to do so. The earlier of the two was his severe wounding during the night of July 8, 1918. The boy was not yet nineteen when he joined an American Red Cross ambulance group stationed near Schio in northern Italy. This was early in June. For nearly a month he drove ambulances carrying wounded men to base hospitals. But this was too tame an occupation; he was spoiling for closer contact with the enemy. Early in July he volunteered to go across to the Piave Front where the Italians faced the Austrians from trenches and dugouts so close to the lines that they could hear one another talking. This would mean action, the boy thought, even though his job was only the rather unspectacular one of handing out cigarettes and bars of chocolate to the troops. When he arrived the front seemed quiet, but he soon got more action than he had bargained for. An Austrian *Minenwerfer*, loaded with metal slugs and scrap iron, made a direct hit on the advanced listening post where Hemingway was practicing his very limited Italian with some of the soldiers. Several men were killed outright; one had his legs severed. Although his own extremities were terribly wounded, Hemingway managed to carry the dying soldier back to the main trench, though as he did so Austrian flares lit the scene and a heavy machine gun opened up at knee level on the staggering boy with his bloody burden. Before his heroic journey was done, he had taken two more slugs in the legs. This was the first of the two soul-shaking experiences which he could never forget, and which he had been trying for ten years to embody in prose fiction.

The second of his memorable experiences was a love affair with an American Red Cross nurse in Milan. Her name was Agnes von Kurowsky. Besides being an excellent and experienced nurse, she was young, pretty, kind, and gay. When the boy was brought at last to the comparative quiet and luxury of the base hospital, Miss von Kurowsky was one of those assigned to his case. It was Hemingway's first adult love affair and he hurled himself into it without caution. He seems to have been wholly unaware of the banality of the situation in which the young war hero falls in love with his nurse. Even if he had thought of it in these terms, he would not have cared in the least. For he had managed to convince himself that he was finally and irrevocably in love.

In spite of the fact that they were often separated for varying intervals during the summer and fall of his recuperation, Hemingway saw as much of his nurse as regulations (and competition from his fellow-Americans) would allow. When he sailed for New York in January 1919, his head was full of plans to get a newspaper job, save some money, bring his girl back to the United States, and be married. The traumatic aspect of this experience was that his plans were smashed. After some soul-searching of her own, Agnes decided that it would be a mistake to let a wartime romance try to attain the settled actuality of a peacetime marriage. She was older than he, she was an excellent and dedicated nurse, and she was not at all sure that she wanted to give up so important a profession in order to become another American housewife. Hemingway had not been home very long when he received the letter in which she set forth her conclusions.

It was a severe blow to his pride. He reacted explosively. All her protestations availed nothing. He turned against her with masculine rage and rankling sorrow, even as he had turned toward her while he lay recuperating in the hospital. But he was never able or willing to forget her. Though he subsequently married four times, he kept Agnes' letters all his life. Among the many he had loved and won, she was a perennial reminder of one woman he had loved and lost. She took on the not very enviable status of the goddess who is worshipped while remaining unattainable. As the first love of his young manhood, she remained enshrined in an alcove of his consciousness until the day he died.

To leave the impression that it is merely fictionized autobiography would be unfair to Hemingway's novel. It is far more artfully imagined and put together, for example, than *The Sun Also Rises,* the first novel, which was built directly upon his remembrance of the people he knew and the events he was witness to during the summertime visit to Pamplona in 1925.

One distinguishing mark of *A Farewell to Arms,* as against *The Sun Also Rises,* is that Hemingway's powers of invention were called much more intensively into play. To take one example, the time segment covered in the action of the novel runs from the summer of 1916 to the spring of 1918—many months before Hemingway himself arrived upon the scene. The famous account of the retreat from Caporetto, which the author himself always insisted upon calling the retreat from the Isonzo, was never part of his own experience. It had to be invented ex post facto from a study of contemporaneous newspaper stories and the few military histories then available, supplemented and highlighted by Hemingway's own adventures in a very different section of the world when he was a foreign correspondent covering the retreat of Greek soldiers and civilians in Thrace and Anatolia during the fall of 1922.

Another typical instance of Hemingway's inventiveness is the figure of Catherine Barkley, the English nurse who serves as tragic heroine of the story. The character of Catherine is based, not only on the nurse, Agnes von Kurowsky, but is also a composite portrait of Hemingway's first two wives. He seeks to disguise this fact by changing his heroine's nationality and by causing her to speak in an imitation of British upper-class idiom. But when the nurse and her lover go to live far away from the black tides of war in a Swiss chalet high above the city of Lausanne, Hemingway is clearly recalling his visits to the same region with his first wife, Hadley Richardson, as well as the skiing trips he made with her to the mountain village of Schruns in the Austrian Vorarlberg during three winters in the middle 1920's. Finally, it is at least an educated surmise that the idea of having Catherine Barkley die in childbirth following an unsuccessful Caesarean section was suggested to Hemingway by the fact that his second wife, Pauline Pfeiffer, had a difficult time from the same cause in 1928, just when Hemingway was composing the final chapters of the first draft of his novel.

None of this is very surprising. Any novelist must write from what he knows, taking advantage of the hints and suggestions that fall into his lap by chance. Hemingway's real artistic triumph in *A Farewell to Arms* was the way in which he developed various kinds of natural symbolism to sustain and enrich the story over which he had been brooding for ten years. In moving now to the symbolic aspects of the book, I am fully aware that to many readers the very idea of symbolism is anathema. Such readers will tell you that they like their stories straight, and that we are dealing here with a simple naturalistic tale about a pair of young people, thrown together by chance in the midst of a war they never made. They meet, fall in love, and are separated by vast events beyond their control. When they reunite and run away together, they manage to live for a time in circumstances that are certainly pleasurable and apparently ideal. But the fist of fate is poised to crush them. In the end the girl dies and her lover is left to carry on alone.

Hemingway once called his novel a version of the Romeo and Juliet story. There are of course a thousand points of difference between Shakespeare's drama of civil warfare between the Montagues and the Capulets and Hemingway's account of the good and ill fortunes of another pair of starcrossed lovers. What links the two stories is the carefully wrought sense of foreboding—our constantly growing awareness of a looming fatefulness at work behind the scenes. Our skeptical reader may well argue that such a literary parallelism is enough: we need no supplementary symbolism to convince us of the drama and the pathos of the story. Hemingway felt otherwise. For the symbolism is there, and it got there only through the most careful planning and the most extensive rewriting. Let us turn to three phases of the symbolism to see what Hemingway did with them.

Symbolic effects in this novel are achieved through a subtle process of reiterated suggestion. Among the many which might be mentioned, we shall be concerned with only three: the weather, the emblematic people, and the landscapes. The best known of these is the first: the almost poetic care with which Hemingway slowly builds up in his readers a mental association between rain and disaster. This was an association which came naturally enough to Hemingway himself. His letters throughout his life are full of complaints against rain and damp weather. He always took it personally, partly because he was susceptible to the common cold, partly because damp dark weather induced in his spirit a comparable gloom. Moreover, in his second experience of war and its effects, he had personally watched the pitiful stream of refugees plodding through mud and sodden with rain during the memorable evacuation of the civilian population from the city of Adrianople. Anyone who reads *A Farewell to Arms* with one eye on the weather will eventually marvel as he watches the author playing with falling rain as a symbol of imminent doom. Near the close of the book, when Catherine is approaching her time of confinement, the weather warms and the rains arrive. For a whole miraculous winter the lovers have gloried in their isolation, living happily in their high mountain fastness, surrounded by healthy cold air and clean snow, far from the mud and muck of war. Now at last the rains come, the time for the lying-in draws near, some great change lurks just beyond the lovers' limited horizon, and we begin to sense that Catherine is in mortal danger, as indeed she is.

A second aspect of the symbolism is the way in which Hemingway endows two of Lieutenant Henry's friends with special moral attributes. One is the young Italian surgeon, Rinaldi, a merry comrade and a capable doctor, enthusiastic about his work with the wounded, boasting of his attainments at the operating table, delighted to be of service to humanity. But Hemingway is at pains to present Rinaldi as the victim of his own virtues. The sadness and fatigue of war soon affect him. As we watch, he becomes the homeless man, without visible antecedents, cut off from saving domesticity, driven to desperate expedients in order to keep his sanity in the vast and gloomy theatre of the war. Trying to relax from the rigors of his duties, he contracts syphilis in an army brothel. The man of science is eventually victimized by the filth and disease which surround him.

The second close friend is a nameless Italian priest, a gentle little nut-brown man who seeks as well as he can to exemplify the Christian virtues in a situation where almost everything seems to conspire against them. It is he who tries to persuade Henry to visit the Abruzzi during one of his military leaves. The priest paints an idyllic picture of this mountainous region, with its clear cool air, its plump game birds, its vineyards and orchards, its flute music, its peasant population living simply and amicably as they have done for a thousand years. It is a region close to heaven—or at any rate closer than the Veneto would seem to be. "There," says the priest, "a man may love God without being satirized for his beliefs."

After the first half of the novel, Rinaldi and the priest disappear from the scene. But the qualities they stand for continue to affect the action of the story. When Henry and Catherine reach Switzerland and begin the only approximation of married life that they will ever know, it is the spirit of the priest which dominates their lives. When, on the other hand, they are compelled to leave their lofty station and descend to Lausanne, where Catherine will die, we are forcibly reminded of the world of Rinaldi—the world of doctors and hospitals and imminent death.

The third and last manifestation of symbolic intent in the novel is the subtle way in which the author plays off two levels of landscape against each other. Without following it slavishly, he carefully establishes a pattern in which plains or lowlands are associated in the reader's mind with war, death, pain, sadness, or gloom, while the high mountain regions, whether in the Abruzzi where the priest originated, or in Switzerland, high above Lausanne, where the lovers establish their temporary heartland, are just as carefully associated with pleasure and the good life, joy and health, or whatever stands opposed to the plains of the Veneto where the war is being fought and the great retreat has been made. This poetic association of the heights with pleasure and the depths with pain is Hemingway's version of the *paysage moralise,* the moralized landscape which he was teaching himself to use as a backdrop for his narratives of action.

In sum, we are suggesting that *A Farewell to Arms* is not at all the naturalistic report which we might at first take it for. One of the major reasons for its continuing freshness, its proven power of survival, is the care which Hemingway lavished on its structure and texture by the symbolic use of weather and character and moralized landscape.

As we approach the end of this demonstration, there is just time to consider one more point about *A Farewell to Arms.* This is the famous conclusion where Catherine dies and her lover says a silent farewell before he walks back to the hotel alone in the falling rain. For years it has been rumored that Hemingway rewrote the closing pages of the novel some thirty-seven times. The figure is very likely exaggerated. But whatever it was, there can be no doubt that Hemingway spent considerable effort on the conclusion, and that the final version, familiar to readers since 1929, is almost infinitely superior to the penultimate version, which has only recently come to light.

In the accepted and familiar version, Hemingway's hero stays with Catherine until her death. Then he goes out to speak to the surgeon: "Is there anything I can do tonight?" The doctor replies that there is nothing to be done and offers Henry a ride back to his hotel. Henry says that he will stay for a while at the hospital. "It was the only thing to do," says the surgeon, apologetically, speaking of the fatal Caesarean section. "The operation proved—"

"I do not want to talk about it," says Henry. The doctor goes away down the corridor and Henry opens the door to the room where Catherine's body lies.

"You can't come in now," says one of the nurses in charge.

"Yes, I can."

"You can't come in yet."

"You get out," says Henry. "The other one, too."

But after he has got them out and closed the door and turned off the light, he discovers that it is no good. It is like saying good-bye to a statue. After a while he goes out and leaves the hospital, and walks back to the hotel in the rain.

This is where the novel ends. Much has been made of this justly famous and tight-lipped conclusion. To many readers it has seemed to be one of the high points of lonely bereavement in modern fiction, a peak of tragic lostness from a generation which suffered thousands of similar deprivations during and after World War I. It has also been seen as the epitome of stoic acceptance of the inevitable. There can be no doubt that this was precisely the effect Hemingway sought to achieve during all his rewritings of the conclusion.

The penultimate version is another matter entirely, and it is very revealing. In place of the laconic interchange between Henry and the attending surgeon, the visit to the room to say goodbye, and the lonely walk back to the hotel in the rain, we have three quite different paragraphs. Henry talks about the difficulty of making funeral arrangements in a foreign country, then of the postwar destinies of the priest and Rinaldi and one or two more, and finally of the return to the hotel, where he falls asleep to awake in the morning to his sense of loss. All the sharp poignancy of the final version is here blunted and destroyed. What is worse, the words themselves seem moist with self-pity.

Hemingway wrote, in the simulated character of Frederic Henry:

There are a great many more details, starting with my first meeting with an undertaker, and all the business of burial in a foreign country, and going on with the rest of my life—which has gone on and seems likely to go on for a long time.

I could tell how Rinaldi was cured of the syphilis and lived to find that the technic learned in wartime surgery is not of much practical use in peace. I could tell how the priest in our mess lived to be a priest in Italy under Fascism. I could tell how Ettore became a Fascist and the part he took in that organization. I could tell how Piani got to be a taxi-driver in New York and what sort of a singer Simmons became. Many things have happened. Everything blunts and the world keeps on. It never stops. It only stops for you. Some of it stops while you are still alive. The rest goes on and you go on with it.

I could tell you what I have done since March, 1918, when I
walked that night in the rain back to the hotel where Catherine
and I had lived and went upstairs to our room and undressed
and slept finally, because I was so tired—to wake in the morning
with the sun shining in the window; then suddenly to realize
what had happened. I could tell what has happened since then,
but that is the end of the story.

The difficulty with this conclusion is that it drowns us with
words and moisture. The rather garrulous self-pity, so visible here,
when we juxtapose it with the far more objective stoicism of the
final version, offers us a hint that may be worth developing. It
suggests what I believe to be true, that the stoicism of the last
version was only a mask, adopted and assumed for dramatic show,
while under it Hemingway's still wounded feelings were bleeding
and suppurating almost as intensively as they had been doing ten
years before. Within the short space of seven months, he had been
badly smashed up in both war and love. Now, much later, his
double wound of body and soul rose to the surface of his memory,
and manifested itself in the trial conclusion which we have just
examined.

There is no time to expand further upon the matters here. Yet
the idea of the stoic mask, assumed as a facade to conceal the
psychic warfare which is going on beneath, may help us to explain
and to understand much of the braggadoccio which struck his
detractors as all too apparent in Hemingway's later life. It may
also explain his espousal of the stoic code as a standard of behavior
—a standard to which he required all his later heroes to conform.
But these are hypotheses better suited to the biographer than to
the literary critic. If the next-to-last conclusion of *A Farewell to
Arms* betrays a kind of psychological quicksand just below the
surface, the final version does not. It is still as firm and fresh as
the brook pebbles which Ford Madox Ford so much admired.
Whatever Hemingway's future reputation, *A Farewell to Arms*
will surely stand for at least another forty years as the best novel
written by an American about the First World War.

James F. Light

The Religion of Death in
A Farewell to Arms

One way of looking at Ernest Hemingway's *A Farewell to Arms*
is to see its close involvement in four ideals of service.[1] Each of
these ideals is dramatized by a character of some importance, and
it is between these four that Lt. Henry wavers in the course of
the novel. The orthodoxly religious ideal of service is that of the
Priest, who wishes to serve God but who asserts as well the broader
concept of service: "When you love you wish to do things for. You
wish to sacrifice for. You wish to serve."[2] Another selfless ideal of

---

ction of *Farewell*. Anyone familiar with Mr. Warren's essay will see that
though I disagree with much of its interpretation of *Farewell,* I at the same
time am indebted to it deeply.

[2] Ernest Hemingway, *A Farewell to Arms,* Intro. Robert Penn Warren
(Scribner's Modern Standard Authors, 1949), p. 75. Subsequent page
references to *Farewell* are from this edition and are incorporated in the
text.

service is that of the patriot Gino, who wishes to serve his country
so fully that he is willing to die for it. A third is the code of
Catherine Barkley, who wishes to serve her lover and who sees in
such service her personal substitute for conventional religion. The
last is the ideal of Rinaldi, who, as a doctor, wishes to serve mankind by alleviating the wounds of war. Each is an initiate to the
subordination of self, and in this they differ from the selfishness
of the king and the officers who ride in cars and throw mud on the
men, or from the hero Ettore, who sees war as an accident suitable
for promotion and self-glorification. In no other way, despite the
contention of such a perceptive and influential critic as Robert
Penn Warren, are they really initiates. They are not so in their
greater discipline—Catherine is hysterical early in the novel and
Rinaldi is a nervous wreck in the middle. They are not so in their
talk, for though Rinaldi and Valentini, another doctor and another
so-called initiate, may possess a similar "bantering, ironical tone,"
the Priest and Catherine are far removed from any such tone; nor
do they have any greater awareness than others "of the issue of
meaning in life."[3] They act instinctively rather than intellectually,
and the one instinct they have in common—the attraction toward
the ideal of service—is, from the context and the conclusion of the
novel, a foolish selflessness without intellectual worth.

The Priest, Gino, Catherine, and Rinaldi do, however, live by
the ideal of service, and the dramatic tension of the novel is largely
based on Lt. Henry's wavering toward each ideal and eventual
rejection of all four. Toward the Priest's ideal, Henry's attitude
is at first one of sympathy but of rejection. He does not bait the
Priest with the other priest-baiters early in the novel, but neither
does he stay with the Priest when the other officers leave for the
whore houses near by. Nor does he visit the high, cold, dry country, the Priest's home, where he is invited to go on his leave.
Instead he goes to the large cities, the ironic "centres of culture
and civilization" (p. 8), where he lives the life of sensation and
feels "that this was all and all and all and not caring" (p. 13).
After he is wounded and has found real love with Catherine, however, Lt. Henry comes closer to the Priest, so that when he returns
to duty he can reject the priest-baiting of Rinaldi and instead of
going to town—and the whore houses—he can visit with the
Priest. The implication apparently is that the love Henry has
found in Catherine has somehow made him more sympathetic to
the kind of selfless love that the Priest avows. By the end of the

---

[3] Warren, Introduction to Hemingway's *A Farewell to Arms,* p. xxxi.

novel, however, Henry has thoroughly rejected the Priest and his ideal of service to God. He does, however, give that ideal a test. Where the Priest had earlier prayed for the end of the war—"I believe and I pray that something will happen. I have felt it very close" (pp. 184-5).—Henry now prays that Catherine not die. Basic and repetitive in the prayer is the implication of some necessary reciprocal relation between man and God: you do this for me and I'll do this for you. Thus Henry prays: "Oh, God, please don't let her die. I'll do anything for you if you won't let her die. . . . Please, please, please don't let her die. . . . I'll do anything you say if you don't make her die" (p. 341). Catherine, however, does die, just as, despite the Priest's prayers, the war continues. The implication is that the Priest's ideal of service lacks reciprocity, and the knowledge of its lack is not unique to Henry. Huck Finn had earlier, in the novel that Hemingway has said is the origin of all modern American literature, felt the same flaw; for he had seen, by pragmatic test, the inefficacy of prayer, and he had discerned that the Priest's—or Miss Watson's—ideal of service was a one-way street with no advantage for the human individual. For Lt. Henry this lack of reciprocity makes for the image of a God who in his eternal selfishness is the origin of human selfishness, so that man in his selfishness most accurately reflects God. This concept of the divine selfishness is portrayed in Henry's remembrance, as Catherine is dying, of watching some ants burning on a log. Henry envisions the opportunity for him to be "a messiah and lift the log off the fire" (p. 339). Divinity, however, does not ease the pain of man's existence, and Henry does not save the ants. Instead, selfishly—and in so doing he is reflecting the divine selfishness which is so antithetical to the Priest's ideal of service—Henry throws "a tin cup of water on the log, so that I would have the cup empty to put whiskey in before I added water to it" (p. 339).

A second ideal of service is that dramatized by the patriot Gino. He believes the "soil is sacred" (p. 190) and that the deaths in the war were not "in vain" (p. 191). He will not talk of losing the war and Lt. Henry feels he understands Gino's "being a patriot. He was born one" (p. 191). Though Lt. Henry never has Gino's simple love of country, he does for a good part of the novel act and talk as a "patriot." The priest applies the term to Lt. Henry (p. 74), and its justification, despite the fact that Lt. Henry is not defending his own country, is shown in an early conversation of Lt. Henry with the mechanic Passini. Passini believes there is nothing worse than war, but Lt. Henry contradicts this by saying, "Defeat is worse" (p. 52). Passini says people should defend their own homes, and sisters should be kept in the house. The disagreement concludes with Lt. Henry saying that the war is bad but it must be finished. Passini answers, "It doesn't finish. There is no finish to a war" (p. 52). The innocence of Lt. Henry is revealed when he says, "Yes, there is" (p. 52). In terms of the ultimate despair of the book, with its cry that life itself, from birth to death, is perpetual war, Lt. Henry's statement shows a naivete that Lt. Henry must—and does—lose. His loss begins when the real danger and killing of the war become apparent. (Earlier he had felt the war "seemed no more dangerous to me myself than war in the movies" [p. 38].) His loss of innocence is most obvious when he feels himself completely separated from the patriot Gino and responds to Gino's cliches by the famous passage that begins, "I was always embarrassed by the words sacred, glorious, and sacrifice, and the expression in vain . . ." (p. 191). Because he has lost his patriotism, Lt. Henry, later, has no intellectual qualms about deserting and making a "separate peace" (p. 252).

A third ideal of service is the ideal of which Catherine lives. She dramatizes the service of secular lovers to one another, and she lives and dies by this code. Completely selfless in her attitude toward her lover, she needs no marriage ceremony and dreams of uniting herself so completely to Lt. Henry—her religion she calls him at one time—that the two become truly one. The depth of the desire to serve is shown in the last chapter. There, Lt. Henry takes Catherine's hand. She knows that she is going to die and also feels that her recent agony in childbirth and her impending death are the final results for her of the sexual desires of Henry. Therefore, she lashes out: "Don't touch me" (p. 341). Then, despite her bitterness, she adds, "Poor darling. You touch me all you want" (p. 342). This is perfect selflessness, still concerned with others, still trying to serve even while dying, and it is this kind of service that Henry learns about from Catherine. Thus while rowing Catherine to Switzerland, Henry can blister his hands to the point of real pain, and then can jestingly refer to his own hands as similar to those of Christ. Later, when Catherine is dying, Henry desperately wishes to serve, and this he does in some small way by giving her gas to ease her pain. Of this act, he feels, "It was very good of the doctor to let me do something" (p. 328). Later Henry asks such questions as, "Do you want anything, Cat?" and "Can I get you anything?" (p. 342). Henry, however, can do nothing, and the ineffectuality of the service of secular lovers is made apparent in the last paragraph of the novel when Henry finds he can't even effectively say goodbye.

The fourth ideal of service is that of Rinaldi. Rinaldi is a good doctor, one for whom work is the sole justification for life. It is Rinaldi to whom Henry is closest at the beginning of the novel—Rinaldi says they are blood brothers—for both are not only living a life of non-thinking sensation, but more important both are involved in the service of healing man's body. After Henry has been wounded and has returned to duty, however, there is a change. Henry finds that the Priest now is more sure of himself, while Rinaldi, convinced that he has syphilis, is tense and irritable. The cause for the change is the way in which the war has been going. Many men have been killed and many wounded, and these facts have made the Priest—concerned with man's soul—feel more necessary, while at the same time, they have made Rinaldi—concerned with man's body—feel his own futility. The difference is made clear when Rinaldi attempts to bait the priest, as in earlier days, and is unsuccessful in weakening the Priest's placidity. His lack of success, though his insults go even beyond those of the earlier time, and his feeling that Henry is betraying him and is now on the Priest's side enrage Rinaldi, and he yells at Henry that he can't side with the Priest: "You can't do it. You can't do it. I say you can't do it. You're dry and you're empty and there's nothing else. There's nothing else I tell you. Not a damned thing. I know, when I stop working" (p. 180). The complete materialist—he calls himself "the snake of reason" (p. 176)—Rinaldi, after this scene, disappears physically from the novel, but his role as the worker for the cure of man's body is assumed later by another doctor, the one who cares for Catherine in her childbirth. Like Rinaldi, this doctor is also ineffectual in his attempt at service, and his feeling of his failure leads to apologies which Henry rejects. Henry is left with the failure of all the ideals of service. In addition he is left with the knowledge of the one thing man can believe in: death. Catherine becomes a "statue"—which suggests some pagan deity—and the novel ends on the word *rain*, a word which symbolically stands for two things, paradoxically intertwined, in the novel. One is spring and new birth. The other is the thaws of spring that begin the war anew and anew bring death. In the beginning of life, then, is the fact of death, and the sexual urge is the biological trap which leads to death. Death is the basic fact of life.

The imagery of the novel, from beginning to end, insists upon the tragic fusion of birth and destruction—as, for instance, in the first chapter, in which the cartridge boxes of marching soldiers make their capes bulge so that the mud-bedraggled warriors "Marched as though they were six months gone with child" (p. 4). Or Hemingway makes the same point, through images with Freudian sexual overtones, when he has Lt. Henry, while walking with Catherine, stop to buy a gun, holster it, comment upon his now being "fully armed" (p. 149), and then takes his beloved to a hotel to enjoy the "good destruction"—a common phrase of the two lovers—before he must return to a different kind of destruction at the front. Or most poignantly the fused imagery of birth and death is dramatized by a single image of Catherine's child: the birth cord, as Lt. Henry imagines, is around its neck and the cord is slowly choking the infant to death from the moment of its first kick inside the mother's body. Such an image evokes man's universal fate, for life itself—as Lt. Henry phrases it—is merely "all this dying to go through" (p. 327).

It is no wonder that in Hemingway's next book, *Death in the Afternoon,* he states—and it is a thorough rejection of any ideal of service—that "what is moral is what you feel good after and what is immoral is what you feel bad after."[4] Hemingway feels good after seeing a bullfight, and for him it is "very moral."[5] The reason is that in the bullfight one confronts in a pure way the ultimate fact of death. Man's problem is to dominate death as the bullfighter's is to dominate the bull, and the way toward domination is to see life, like the bullfight, as an art form, with certain rules which the "manly" man will obey. The basic offense against the "rules" of the bullfight is for the bullfighter to pretend to be in the area of danger while in reality he avoids that area and is perfectly safe. The basic offense against the "rules" of life as an art form is to show self-pity, an offense so great that Hemingway could, when he saw it in his friend Scott Fitzgerald, write a reprimanding letter in which he pointed out that all men "are bitched from the start" and no man has any right to whine.[6] To avoid the area of danger in the bullfight is to avoid real domination of the bull; to whine in life is to avoid domination of death. The lack of domination makes for messiness—impure art—in either the bull-

[4] Ernest Hemingway, *Death in the Afternoon* (Scribner's, 1932), p. 4.
[5] Hemingway, *Death in the Afternoon,* p. 4.
[6] Letter from Ernest Hemingway to F. Scott Fitzgerald. Quoted in Arthur Mizener, *The Far Side of Paradise* (Houghton-Mifflin, 1951), p. 238.

fight or life. Such messiness is a form of cheating, and in life "when you get the damned hurt use it—don't cheat with it."[7]

Watching the bullfights, Hemingway gains a feeling of "life and death, mortality and immortality."[8] Though he himself is vague about the reason.he gains these feelings, it seems clear that the feeling of immortality does not come from any orthodox Christian reason. Instead it arises because the bullfighter, when he enters the area of danger, shows his contempt for death, becomes victorious over it, and gains in his victory a small immortality. The same kind of contempt for death is evident in the way in which Catherine meets her end, for she recognizes her death as a "dirty trick" (p. 342) but winks at the joke. She has not been broken by death, despite her feeling to the contrary, and she has therefore gained victory and immortality. This is the only kind of immortality man can know; it is gained by bravery and stoicism, not selfless service to God (the Priest), country (Gino), beloved (Catherine), or mankind (Rinaldi). Such a limited immortality is a poor substitute for victory over death through everlasting life; but it is the only kind of immortality, the only kind of religion, the Hemingway of *Farewell* can believe in.

---

[7] Letter from Hemingway to Fitzgerald. Quoted in Mizener, *The Far Side of Paradise,* p. 238.
[8] Hemingway, *Death in the Afternoon,* p. 4.

Otto Friedrich

Ernest Hemingway: Joy Through Strength

It was in *A Farewell to Arms* that Hemingway first achieved a structurally coherent novel expressing his own values, and two of his three subsequent novels were largely devoted to rewriting and repeating the same idea. Death appears at the very start when Hemingway sets the scene and sounds a muted fanfare:

> Troops went by the house and down the road and the dust they raised powdered the leaves of the trees. . . . Sometimes in the dark we heard the troops marching under the window and guns going past pulled by motor-tractors. . . . At the start of the winter came the permanent rain and with the ᵣ⁻ ˙ ne the cholera. But it was checked and in the end ⌐ᵣ' nd died of it in the army.

Love ap, ᵤt Frederic Henry meets
Catherine ᵢ ʳ first meeting is spent
in unpleasa, , Henry gets his face
slapped, but ᵢt "I'd be glad to kiss
you if you d ↄtherine promptly de-

⌐ This excerpt is ....erican *Scholar,* XXVI (Autumn,
1957), 519-524. . ↄermission of the author and publisher.

mands: "You will be good to me, won't you?" The third meeting, after an absence of a few days, takes us even further into fantasy:

"Say, 'I've come back to Catherine in the night.' "
"I've come back to Catherine in the night."
"Oh, darling, you have come back, haven't you?"
"Yes."

There is only the briefest transition between this comic-opera "front" and the real front, where an enlisted man tells Henry, "There is nothing worse than war. . . . What is defeat? You go home." It is not a concentration of effect, but a violent leap into another world. Henry and his men are eating cheese when they are hit by a shell.

> There was a flash. . . . I tried to breathe but my breath would not come and I felt myself rush bodily out of myself and out and out and out and all the time bodily in the wind. I went out swiftly, all of myself and I knew I was dead and that it was a mistake to think you just died. Then I floated, and instead of going on I felt myself slide back. . . . I thought somebody was screaming. . . . When I touched him he screamed. His legs . . . were both smashed above the knee.

This electric moment, which apparently re-enacts the wound Hemingway suffered at the age of eighteen, brings us back to the world of Ambrose Bierce. ("He stooped and laid his hand upon its face. It screamed.") But where Bierce was driven to relive his years of horror over and over, Hemingway withdraws again to the rear lines. Lieutenant Henry, the most numb of all Hemingway's heroes, makes no reflections on his experiences as he suffers himself to be carried back to a hospital, and the war recedes into the background as abruptly as it emerged.

Hemingway's best war stories—and war is really rather remote in almost all of Hemingway—deal not with the actual fighting but with the memories and aftereffects of fighting. Perhaps the best, "A Way You'll Never Be," describes Nick Adams wandering in a state of shell shock, refusing to wear a helmet because "I've seen them full of brains too many times." "In Another Country" is set in a hospital and begins with the statement that "the war was always there, but we did not go to it any more." Krebs, in "Soldiers Home," has suffered a more quiet and perhaps more permanent shell shock than Nick: "He did not want any consequences.

He did not want any consequences ever again. He wanted to live along without consequences."

In *A Farewell to Arms*, Catherine Barkley appears at the hospital. Presto. "When I saw her I was in love with her. Everything turned over inside of me." This is the matter-of-fact approach for which Hemingway is famous. You are dead. Then you are not dead. You see a girl, your insides turn over, and you are in love. From then on, Catherine Barkley never talks about anything but love and sex, and talks interminably of these in the same kittenish way. ("You've such a lovely temperature.")

Catherine is one of Hemingway's most unreal creations and one of his most typical, for she represents an attempt to personify a false ideal. Many other writers—Hawthorne is an extreme example—have risked similar attempts, but the risk lies less in the method itself than in the quality of the ideal. Hawthorne, for example, could convey a kind of reality through Hester Prynne by the intensity with which he felt the idea of expiation. Fielding's atempts to personify the ideal woman provide a closer analogy, yet the quality of the ideal again makes an immeasurable difference. Amelia Booth, for instance, almost too wonderful, remains faithful to an unfaithful husband, raises money to pay his debts, beats off seducers, raises a swarm of children, and remains unfailingly charming. Stendhal's ideal woman, the Duchess of Sanseverina, is equally extraordinary, in a more grandiose and less domestic way.

Any heroine suffers by comparison, but Catherine Barkley suffers particularly because of the tawdriness of the ideal that she personifies only too well. On the last night of Henry's convalescent leave in Milan, he takes her to the inevitable hotel and she complains that "I've never felt like a whore before." Politely reassured that she is not a whore, she revives: "I'm a good girl again." The nothingness of Catherine Barkley was finally expressed in her announcement that "there isn't any me. I'm you." Robert Jordan had a similar suspicion that his dream girl might be "like the dreams you have when someone you have seen in the cinema comes to your bed at night and is so kind and lovely." Colonel Cantwell pushes this nothingness to its conclusion in *Across the River and Into the Trees* when he avows his love to Renata's portrait and even hears the picture answer back. The picture, after all, is no less real than Renata, another "someone you have seen in the cinema."

Henry, as a hero, is scarcely less vague, too passive to dominate the narrative, too unreflective to serve as observer. He is the K. of

Hemingway's universe, the central cipher. He is typical in disguising his inadequacy by a meaningless worldliness. ("We drank a bottle of Capri and a bottle of St. Estephe.") Even when the hero is unheroic, the arcana of wines and foreign revolvers, street names in remote cities and special ways to catch fish, identify him as a man who has lived. They imply, as insistently as a black eyepatch, that he is stronger and wiser for his sufferings. An even more extreme example is Harry, the writer-hero of "The Snows of Kilimanjaro," dying of gangrene on a hunting expedition to Africa, bickering with the wife who supports him, and agonizing over "the things that he had saved to write until he knew enough to write them well." The catalogue of his unexploited treasures is so completely trivial that it is hard to believe the critics who consider the story autobiographical. One item is described only as playing cards in a blizzard, another is a tiresome anecdote about love quarrels and a whore in Constantinople. There are undeveloped bits about trout fishing, about poverty in Paris, a murder by a half-wit, a man being hit by a bomb. Harry complains because his wife "dulled his ability and softened his will to work."

The whole story, as a matter of fact, had already been written somewhat better by Henry James a half century earlier. The tragedy of realization too late for achievement obsessed James all his life, and he compressed into *The Middle Years* a semiautobiographical version of the idea that subsequently inspired both *The Ambassadors* and *The Wings of the Dove*. It was typical of James that he left implicit, in *The Middle Years*, what Dencombe had written or might have written. James made Dencombe's problem both simpler and more significant:

> What he saw so intensely today, what he felt as a nail driven in, was that only now, at the very last, had he come into possession. His development had been abnormally slow, almost grotesquely gradual. He had been hindered and retarded by experience, he had for long periods only groped his way. . . . At such a rate a first existence was too short—long enough only to collect material; so that to fructify, to use the material, one should have a second age, an extension.

The imminence of death brings Dencombe to an intense understanding of his crisis. He comes to realize that the universal belief in a little more time is as illusory as the idea of a "second existence." He realizes, in short, his own mortality, and his heightened understanding inspires his outcry: "A second chance—that's the

delusion. There never was to be but one. We work in the dark—
we do what we can—we give what we have. Our doubt is our
passion and our passion is our task. The rest is the madness of
art." Hemingway's protagonist, who never finally understands
anything, addresses his last words to the figure of death. " 'You've
got a hell of a breath,' he told it. 'You stinking bastard.' "

With a similar feeling toward the war, Lieutenant Henry leaves
his mistress and heads back to the front. A major in his unit tells
him, "It's been a bad summer." Hemingway skillfully concentrates
the effects of the campaign in the disintegration of Henry's friend,
Rinaldi: "All summer and all fall I've operated. I work all the
time. . . . I never think. No, by God, I don't think; I operate. . . .
This is a terrible war, baby." Rinaldi's surgery also emphasizes
the catastrophe of the retreat from Caporetto, implying the same
futile agony as the cholera that followed the marching men in the
beginning. The retreat is a perfect subject for Hemingway's pictorial method, a somber mural of a defeated army moving through
mud and rain. Hemingway's slow, careful description, with its
emphasis on physical detail, is one of his triumphs.

But such mass movement is unbearable for a Hemingway hero,
and Henry soon cuts across country, stopping to pick up two stragglers. When he gets stuck in a muddy road miles from nowhere,
the two stragglers decide to go off on foot. Henry implies that they
are deserting and calmly shoots them. This murder, which both
Henry and Hemingway seem to consider an admirable act of
justice, is an interesting prophecy of Henry's own fate. He is soon
seized by some battle police who are executing retreating officers
more or less at random. With the roles reversed, Henry retains
his sense of moral outrage. Instead of denouncing the stragglers'
lack of code, he now denounces "the efficiency, coldness and command of themselves, of Italians who are firing and not being fired
on." Death, for the first time, is predictable, and one might think
that the Hemingway hero would face the firing squad, in all its
meaninglessness, with the disdainful smile of a Walter Mitty. But
Henry, in this crisis, acts very humanly, flees, jumps in a river and
swims to safety, buoyed up by his indignation and the morality of
sauve-qui-peut. Symbolic critics have wallowed in the secret meanings of this desertion and flight—it is the cleansing by water, the
baptismal rebirth, the purification for love or the return to the
womb-symbol of life—but Henry himself states his new position
with the same matter-of-fact simplicity that Hemingway habitually
uses when a complex problem of motivation must somehow be

evaded. "You had no more obligation . . . ," Henry tells himself. "I was not against them. I was through."

Once Henry has made his separate peace, the rest of the novel becomes sheer fantasy. Henry rejoins Catherine, by now well advanced in pregnancy, and they revel in a renewed sense of being "alone against the others." Catherine even congratulates herself complacently on her state of superiority over her best friend: "Think how much we have and she hasn't anything." The police close in, but the fugitives row across the lake to safety in Switzerland. There is more kittenish connubiality in the mountains, but the beginning of labor pains brings us back to the reality of battle again, and the long description of childbirth ends in hemorrhage and death.

Catherine's death, repeatedly anticipated by prophecies of disaster and symbols of death in fertility, still comes as a shock because of its meaninglessness. Why does Catherine die? And why does she die in childbirth? One can speculate that Hemingway wants to demonstrate the meaninglessness of life, but it would obviously be absurd to describe a meaningless world by writing something meaningless. One can speculate, more probably, that Catherine's death is simply the old-fashioned storyteller's conventional way of ending a sad story. One can speculate that Hemingway took a Biercean pleasure in killing off his dream heroine and blaming it on cruel gods. But the unanswered question of why things happen in Hemingway's work is more fundamental. Why was Henry in the war? Why did he desert? Why did he fall in love with Catherine? Or she with him? None of this is ever made clear, and similar questions arise in Hemingway's other novels.

Hemingway was once quoted by a reporter, Lillian Ross, as saying, "I learned to write by looking at paintings in the Luxembourg Museum in Paris." Such a declaration could be taken as posturing—on another occasion he claimed it was the Bible that taught him his trade—but the relationship of painting is very relevant to Hemingway's work, and partly explains the defects of *A Farewell to Arms.* Consider a fairly typical example:

> We drove fast when we were over the bridge and soon we saw the dust of the other cars ahead down the road. The road curved and we saw the three cars looking quite small, the dust rising from the wheels and going off through the trees. We caught them and passed them and turned off on a road that climbed into the hills. . . . We were in the foothills on the near side of the river

and as the road mounted there were the high mountains off to the north with snow still on the tops. I looked back and saw the three cars all climbing, spaced by the interval of their dust. We passed a long column of loaded mules, the drivers walking along beside the mules wearing red fezes. They were Bersaglieri. Beyond the mule train the road was empty and we climbed through the hills and then went down over the shoulder of a long hill into a river valley. There were trees along both sides of the road and through the right line of trees I saw the river, the water clear, fast and shallow. . . .

The passage continues in the same manner, the manner that has been admired for bareness and cleanness and simplicity. It is occasionally called "muscular." The later rhetorical Hemingway is only parody of this. As prose style, however, this specimen is scarcely very interesting. The vocabulary, the structure, the rhythm, are all humdrum. In terms of the development, shape or meaning of the novel, it adds nothing. Its only quality, in fact, is based on criteria of visual arts, of painting or photography. Although it lacks color, it is presumably an accurate description of what one would see if one were driving along that road. It leads the eye, not the mind, along in a certain direction. It picks out details the painter might emphasize, but avoids any reference to nonvisual forms of perception.

Hemingway obsessively repeats his determination to describe what "truly" happened, and his concept of truth is deliberately limited to the observable event, the casting of the trout fly or the shooting of the cabinet ministers, how it was done and what it looked like, what an observer could have seen. Even Hemingway's dialogue, what the observer could have heard, is kept free from any subtlety that might remain unheard beneath the surface of physical reality. At his best, Hemingway often resembles Delacroix, whose detailed studies of love and death explored every visible aspect of what truly happened. Despite every ingenuity of perspective, however, the pictorial technique is almost necessarily limited to surfaces. A woman whose husband has just been hit by a railroad train might look exactly like a long-confined lunatic, and neither the painter nor the photographer could distinguish between the two possible meanings of her expression of agony. The whole concept of causality, involving both reasoning analysis and a time sequence, is beyond their reach. Even the most "non-objective" painter trying to paint an abstract emotion is forced to reduce it to a visible surface. But the primary concern of the writer, unlike the painter or the musician, must be meaning rather than beauty.

Hemingway himself outlined his technical methods, and implied their shortcomings, in *Death in the Afternoon*. He declared that he was having difficulty in "knowing what you really felt rather than what you were supposed to feel," and in putting down "what really happened in action." Now "what you really felt" is not a physical reality that can be painted "truly," because feeling obviously cannot be abstracted in this academic way from its various causes. What does the mystic "really feel" at the moment of ecstasy? Does it come from God? the Devil? hunger? desire? chills? sunstroke? neurosis? What does the artist "really feel" at the moment of creation, or the murderer at the moment of killing, and why? The unsuccessful attempt to describe and explain this in all its complexity is the writer's greatest task—"Our doubt is our passion" —and no other artistic method can even approach it. What you "really feel" is inevitably a combination of what you were supposed to feel, what you thought you felt, what you wanted to feel, what you rebelled against feeling, and an infinity of other reactions to the same stimulus. To simplify this, with crutches like "truly" and "really," is necessarily to oversimplify, and to oversimplify is to mistake and corrupt the whole purpose of writing. The great writer neither simplifies nor complicates but demonstrates the complexity itself. If Shakespeare had cast aside what Hamlet was supposed to feel, or if Dostoevsky had ignored what Stavrogin thought he felt, the result might have been scarcely superior to *A Farewell to Arms*. In American literature, the whole tragedy of *Moby Dick* is concentrated on Ahab's insane misconception of the white whale, the whole greatness of James's last work is based on the realization that motive and illusion are everything.

Reality is not essentially a physical thing, and it cannot be understood solely in terms of visible phenomena. This misconception of reality is the basis of Hemingway's romanticism, and his romantic view of both love and death. His supposed realism actually consists of describing his romantic concepts as though they were real.

A Farewell to Arms is in many ways the prototype of all Hemingway's novels, and the juxtaposition of love and death continues throughout his work. Both themes become such obsessions that they tend to merge into a Wagnerian confusion. Love, in this glow of greenish spotlights, is more intense through the imminence of death, yet helps to bring about death, yet turns death into the climax of the love affair.[1]

[1] For a reply to Friedrich's basic arguments, see Sheldon Grebstein, *American Scholar* XXVII (1958), pp. 229-231.

Charles Vandersee

The Stopped Worlds of Frederic Henry

It is not surprising that undergraduates get their names confused, Henry Fleming and Frederic Henry, the one an Ohio boy mixed up in the Civil War battle of Chancellorsville and the other an American ambulance driver mixed up in the Italian theater of World War I. For though fifty-odd years and an ocean separate the two, much unites them. Innocence-into-experience is the shared rite, blood and injury the badge. Each confronts the dirt and disgust of fields and roads, in passages that famously prove their authors' command of sensuous detail and emotional states. Each man is the focus of his book, a shaped individual, yet each is also a type, a symbol. Fleming in *The Red Badge of Courage* is anonymous man, the soldier who does not know why he fights but finally believes the fight to be good. Henry becomes the borderline nihilist, the cynic whose world has frozen him almost numb, the would-be thinker who takes refuge in examined hedonism as if it were a private art gallery. Importantly, each is a philosopher but only an amateur and clumsy philosopher, conscious of his mind at work but unconscious of its skittishness.

This article was written especially for this collection.

Yet we recognize the two men as fundamentally different. Henry
Fleming's great discovery in May of 1863 in the Virginia countryside is an idea. "The world was a world for him." Frederic Henry's
great discovery in spring 1917 in "that town," a nameless Italian
town, is a woman, Catherine Barkley, who dies one year later
while trying to give birth. Fleming discovers an open world; Henry
confronts a closed world. That is the difference.[1]

Because we are scientists rather than readers, the fault being in
the *Zeitgeist* and not in ourselves, our impulse is to look under the
book as well as in it, for Hemingway's meaning. When we do so,
we find five missing paragraphs about the closed world. This is the
ending of the book that Hemingway rejected in 1929.[2] Judges as
well as scientists, we are likely to wish Hemingway had not hidden
these paragraphs. For as it exists now, the novel ends the way we
have discovered bad movies to end: Catherine's unforeseen death,
and then (in a scene of ostentatious understatement and incon-
clusiveness) the door that shuts, the light that switches off, and
the survivor who walks away in the rain. Hemingway should have
ended with thought instead of scene:

> . . . . Many things have happened. Everything blunts and the
> world keeps on. It never stops. It only stops for you. Some of it
> stops while you are still alive. The rest goes on and you go on
> with it.
>   I could tell you what I have done since March, nineteen
> hundred and eighteen, when I walked that night in the rain back
> to the hotel where Catherine and I had lived and went upstairs
> to our room and undressed and slept finally, because I was so
> tired—to wake in the morning with the sun shining in the window;
> then suddenly to realize what had happened. I could tell what
> has happened since then, but that is the end of the story.[3]

He was afraid of overstatement, afraid that by handing us a key,
"Some of it stops," we would seize it gratefully and say, This is
THE key to the whole story.[4]

---

[1] For a fuller discussion of the difference, going beyond these brief keynote
remarks, see Earle Labor, "Crane and Hemingway: Anatomy of Trauma,"
Renascence, XI (Summer, 1959), 189-196.

[2] The ending that Hemingway finally settled on is the result of 39 tries. See
George Plimpton's interview with Hemingway, *Writers at Work: The Paris
Review Interviews* (Second Series) (New York, 1963), p. 222.

[3] Carlos Baker has published the "original conclusion" to the novel in
Ernest Hemingway: Critiques of Four Major Novels (New York, 1962),
p. 75.

[4] Crane was afraid too. Some editions of *The Red Badge of Courage* print
rejected passages from near the end, where Crane makes glaring the

It is not the only key, and since he left it out of the final version it is an invisible key that we as sensitive readers have to shape in our own minds. For one of the things we realize Hemingway to be saying in this novel is that death establishes compartments in time. *Some* deaths do, that is, and we can understand this better by glancing at Shakespeare's *King Lear*:

> The oldest hath borne most: we that are young
> Shall never see so much, nor live so long.

At the very end of the play Edgar is speaking of the old king, calling attention to time past, to the recent tragic weeks of war and intrigue in which have died not only Lear, but also Cordelia, Goneril, Regan, Edmund, and Gloucester. The frenzy has now subsided, and Edgar feels he must give voice to the distraught emotions of the survivors: "Speak what we feel, not what we ought to say." The time when the dead were alive is past, a separate compartment in time, now closed. The horror of their blindness, their meanness, their sufferings, their deaths, offers no examples to be followed, no heroic pattern to emulate, and no real consolation to survivors or to audience. There is no reason to look back, except briefly, as respect demands. Something of Kent and Edgar has died with the dead. Both men have grievously suffered in body and soul for the welfare of Lear and Gloucester, and it has availed nothing. Since they have given large portions of themselves to the futile lives of parent and master, it can be said of their own world, "some of it stops." But, diminished, they go on. The same is true of Frederic Henry, this book being in a sense equivalent to the speech of Edgar. It is the moving oration that ritually shuts the door on a part of his world that has been both beautiful and terrible. And it does one more thing, which Edgar does not have to do (since the play has done it for him): it gives an account of the process by which this part of his world has ended. So that Frederic Henry is, like Edgar, standing virtually alone at the end of a tragedy, as a man filled with emotion and knowing that the burden is on him to speak something. Unlike Edgar, he chooses to function as formal eulogist and historian, not as mourner. He is careful to speak what he *ought*—to set Catherine in a compart-

---

optimism that is already plain enough. For example: "He [Henry Fleming] was emerged from his struggles, with a large sympathy for the machinery of the universe. With his new eyes, he could see that the secret and open blows which were being dealt about the world with such heavenly lavishness were in truth blessings."

ment of time past and then close it off—rather than speak what
he *feels*. For we sense that he feels bitter anger and grief, and yet
we realize that this feeling is not allowed to intrude into the story.

By the act of telling his story, time past is to be shut away, as
in some safe deposit box that the owner knows he will never return
to. Grief too is shut off, present and future grief, by the act of will
that chooses narrative over outburst, stoic exposition over flowing
lamentation. Causing these two closures, time and grief, is Catherine's death, the shutting off of her life by "them"—the fates, the
unnameables. "They kill us for their sport," Gloucester had decided, thinking of the gods. "They threw you in and told you the
rules and the first time they caught you off base they killed you,"
says Frederic Henry.[5]

There are three portions of Henry's world that come to a stop,
and we have looked at one of them: the blissful time during which
Catherine was present. Let us briefly examine the other two:
Catherine herself and Frederic's grief for Catherine.

She has at first represented a beautiful new world that is opening to Henry, not closing. "I thought I had never seen any one so
beautiful"—this at the Ospedale Maggiore in Milan (95), when
the young American lieutenant knows he is in love with the
British nurse. Then in the summer the world of love opens further
new discoveries. "Besides all the big times we had many small ways
of making love and we tried putting thoughts in the other one's
head while we were in different rooms" (118). It is during this
summer that their baby is conceived, and it is no wonder that
Henry cannot take seriously Rinaldi, the moody military surgeon
who asserts from his own closed world: "We never get anything
new" (177). The love of Catherine *is* new: "We could feel alone
when we were together, alone against the others. It has only
happened to me like that once" (258). Thus the lover in retro-
spect. The world of Catherine is newness, pleasure, and discovery.
Their transient cubicles in hotels and hospitals are designated
"home" (122f., 258). This is the woman whose life closes, with
chilling peripeteia—"Nothing ever happens to the brave" (146)—
just as it should be expanding. Catherine's child is stillborn, and
Catherine herself dies. Where there were three, now there is one.

The third part of Henry's world that stops is grief. Love, when
the recipient is dead and cannot therefore respond to glance or

---

[5] *A Farewell to Arms* (New York, 1929), p. 338. Further references to this
edition are by page number in the text.

touch, has only one medium left, words. But by its very nature
grief is an emotional state for which words are only contamination.
Speech is public, the property potentially of generations and of
millions, while the essence of grief is utterly private and cannot
partake of this dissemination. Emily Dickinson, for example, deals
with this matter as she speaks of the morning after death:

> The sweeping up the heart,
> And putting love away
> We shall not want to use again
> Until eternity.

Words of love and sorrow cannot reach the loved one, and it is
sacrilege to strew them elsewhere. Thus only one of Lear's last
speeches about Cordelia is an outburst of grief. And he is, as
Albany observes, psychologically utterly alone on stage as he cries:

> Why should a dog, a horse, a rat, have life,
> And thou no breath at all?

The mourner, however, can use words in other forms than direct
lament. There is the formal elegy, which deals in personification
and in ideas and symbols. The elegy is a *formula* for grief, a
substitute really; it is not pure grief or an attempt at it. Even
Hamlet, more articulate a young university rebel than many since,
grieves in quiet, in his soliloquies. Only the man who feels deeply,
Eliot has written, experiences the need to hide his feelings. In
those literary works where love is really not love but some sort of
fondness, or where love is a light cloak to be donned now and
again, we expect to see verbalizations of grief. Or, in novels of
sentiment we may expect long and tearful lamentations. But the
love of Frederic for Catherine is no mere cloak and cannot be hung
in a closet of words; neither does the laconic young lieutenant tell
his story as a sentimental romance.

Articulation of grief is thus a possibility denied to Frederic
Henry. What is left? Surely some sort of *formula*, as hinted above,
some sort of verbal construct that will be neither lament nor confession. The acceptable possibility is history, but severely controlled history: history which in certain crucial respects is closed.
The original ending again:

> I could tell you what I have done since. . . . I could tell what
> has happened since then, but that [the death, the walk back to
> the hotel in the rain] is the end of the story.

He has shut out what happened since; even the amount of time
that has passed remains uncertain to us. And we cannot help notic-
ing that he has shut out much of what happened before. How old
was he that year in Italy and Switzerland? Where did he come
from—what parents, what school, what town, what healed scars
or open wounds? Of Henry Fleming at Chancellorsville we know
volumes, when we set him against Frederic Henry. Fleming has a
mother, one of Whitman's earthy people, and Ohio is the country
from which he came. Behind him are a farm and a girl, and we are
not far wrong if we assume that these lie ahead of him also. "The
rest goes on and you go on with it." But the teller of a story is
not obliged to talk about "the rest." It is in fact best excluded
when the tale being told is a tragic one. Thus we see no funeral,
and we do not visit Henry's mind as he struggles with his grief
and decides to write this book. Also irrelevant to the story is
Catherine's past. The three sad pages on her fiance (18-20) are
Henry's hammer blows on the theme of meaningless death as much
as they are exposition of Catherine's past. The history, severely
restricted, has to do only with "that year," "the next year," "that
town," "the British hospital," the American hospital in Milan, the
hotel in Stresa, the rowboat, and "the brown wooden house in the
pine trees on the side of the mountain" (299). Meaning is achieved
by the boundaries imposed around it, and as the boundaries narrow, the intensity of meaning increases. Here Daniel J. Schneider
is surely right as he shows the book to be a "pure poem," a lyric
which excludes the complexity of life, the full roundness of character, the conversations with loose ends, the irrelevant details that
bulk out the "loose and baggy" novels of panoramic realism.[6]
Henry's act of narration is the act of refining, concentrating, dis-
tilling, limiting. It is an act of respect for self as well as a
formulaic tribute to Catherine. For it does enable him to go on with
life. He has not bound up every detail of his whole life with her.
That itself would be falsity, and in following that madness lies. To
identify the whole of one's life with the deceased is to join her in
annihilation. What Henry has shut out of his narrative is important, and the reason for the act of shutting is an act of affirming.
Frederic Henry goes on living. Crushed and diminished, yes. Rev-
erent, yes. But on, nevertheless.

---

[6] "Hemingway's *A Farewell to Arms:* The Novel as Pure Poetry," *Modern
Fiction Studies,* XIV (Autumn, 1968), 283-296.

To Robert Penn Warren, one of its closest readers, *A Farewell to Arms* is "in a sense, a religious book."[7] The Twenties, in the eyes of the sensitive, were a protracted wake. With World War I, civilization and progress seemed to have died. Amid the corpses Frederic Henry is grasping for meaning. We do not have to deny this attempt to explain the mood of the book. But neither does it stand as a comprehensive reading of the book. It may seem odd to say, but in one way the War is almost incidental. For it is by no means the War alone that gives Henry his philosophy. "Myopic empiricism" might sum up his philosophy, insofar as we can grasp it from the pages of his book. He generalizes from his own recent experience, and while his first war and first love are exceedingly rich experiences they are not quite enough to build a world-view upon. And it is a world-principle that Henry is grasping for when he philosophizes that "the very good and the very gentle and the very brave" are killed by the world (259). This is not only a war-principle, though war may be involved when humans are thus destroyed. The war in this book does, by seeming caprice, shut the door on many lives—those of anonymous soldiers and suffering civilians as well as of soldiers known to Henry. To the helpless watcher this caprice cannot help enlarging into a principle, the Lear principle that man's life is cheap as beast's. For Henry, however, the principle is established and confirmed not by the war generally but by Catherine's death specifically. It is Catherine to whom Henry is referring, as he philosophizes grimly and nihilistically.

That is part of what makes us realize that we have a love story —a tragedy of love—rather than a war story alone or else a cold Q.E.D. for Henry's philosophical premise about the futility of life. Whatever our authentic reaction to the book may be (and I am prepared to grant that modern young readers are capable of reading the book quite unmoved), we do not react to the story as if we have merely seen a geometrician prove a theorem or listened to Aesop narrate a moral fable. What we do see, and what Henry expects us to feel, is that a real man has been involved with a real woman, has been hurt, and does not know what else to do except close the door. There is little to be learned from the experience, except insofar as sorrow is inherently instructive, regarding the

---

[7] Introduction to the Modern Standard Authors edition of the novel (Scribner's), p. xxvii.

unfathomable ways of the world. The past needs to be stated, to
be arranged in consecutive order—that is the least and the most
one can do: "Speak what we *ought* to say." And then, turn the
key. For it is *not* better to have loved and lost, but neither is the
door that closes on Catherine a door that closes on Frederic Henry.
The novel cannot, like some somber and moving black-and-white
photograph, hang on either of these statements alone without
looking crooked.

Viewing the novel as Henry's history of Catherine is to place
the love affair at the center, moving the War itself off to the edge.
Perhaps more important, it is also to place Hemingway himself
off to the side and assume that we can involve ourselves with
Frederic and Catherine alone. This is what several critics find
themselves unable to do. Dwight Macdonald, for example, does
not find Frederic Henry a totally convincing narrator: "As long
as the lieutenant and Catherine Barkley are making love and
having 'a good time' together, one is bored and skeptical."[8] Catherine is "not a person but an adolescent daydream." Likewise
Daniel J. Schneider, who believes that Catherine is "not a distinct
character at all but Frederic's bitterness or his desire objectified."[9]
The point at issue here would seem to be the question of why this
story is told. Schneider believes we find the answer by looking at
author rather than narrator: "The artistic problem Hemingway
faced was to find the correlatives for his bitterness." Put differ-
ently, Hemingway's basic purpose in writing the book is to
dramatize an emotion—to devise characters and incidents that
will enable us as readers to say, "This is a novel about bitterness."
All this may be well and good, but it is to venture into scientists'
territory. From this realm the reader must ultimately and finally
return. For we must approach the story as we have it, as if it were
actually written by the bereaved Henry. He is the inescapable
narrator and source, not Hemingway.

In short, while Schneider and others take the *emotion* of the
novel as its starting point—Hemingway's own bitterness and desolation and even nihilism—we ought rather to take the *narrator*,
Frederic Henry, as the starting point. The point of view is his, the
style of narration is his, and the strengths or weaknesses of character portrayal belong to him. Or, for a full interpretation, take
both approaches: the novel as Hemingway's and the story as

---

[8] *Against the American Grain* (New York, 1962), p. 176.
[9] "The Novel as Pure Poetry," p. 290.

Henry's. But do not confuse the two. From Schneider's point of view, Hemingway is to be congratulated for producing a beautiful poem, despite a few weak points. From my point of view, Hemingway is to be congratulated for creating first of all a splendid character (this passionate stoic, this thought-harried anti-intellectual) who in turn is to be congratulated for narrating a superbly-controlled history *and* producing a beautiful poem.

Congratulations aside, this method of starting out with Henry rather than with Hemingway, with narrator rather than with author's mood, offers a logical explanation for what Macdonald objects to as a flaw. He complains that Catherine seems ethereal and unreal. But ought we not expect this? Our narrator, after all, is Henry; the picture of Catherine is in *his* words. And Frederic Henry, unlike Jake Barnes of *The Sun Also Rises* (a professional journalist), is not presented to us as an accomplished wordsmith. Henry does reflect upon language; he knows that he detests hollow rhetoric: sacred, glorious, sacrifice, courage, hallow. And he knows what he wants in their stead: names of rivers and villages, numbers of roads and regiments (191). But on another matter, a matter not of war but love, what are the wrong words and the right words? This matter he does not talk about very much, lest he turn himself from lover into linguist and his reader from sympathizer into anatomist. He is writing controlled history, not trying either to pen a highly personal Rousseauistic confession or conduct a detailed psychological analysis after the fashion of Poe in "Ligeia." He does not even round himself off as a character, therefore. Henry the historian makes Henry the lover look at times flat and grotesque. We have no trouble in recognizing that his struggle is to avoid sentiment and romanticizing, and if he fails sometimes to vivify, we remember too that the writer is a soldier, not a practiced writer. Edmund Wilson, who objects to Henry's own flatness, is rightly countered by another critic who asks us to note that "the distinction is crucial" between the two Henrys, the lover and the historian.[10]

It may very well be that Hemingway asked himself, before writing the book, "How can I tell a story about bitterness?" And that he went on to invent a character named Henry and to draw upon his own experiences in the War as useful raw material. But to reach the heart of the book we then must ask the other question that Hemingway himself must have asked: "How will my char-

---

10 Robert W. Lewis, Jr., *Hemingway on Love* (Austin, Texas, 1965), p. 43.

acter, Frederic Henry, tell his story?" When we ask this, we get answers that we would otherwise not get. We begin to understand how those philosophizing passages function—the interpolations which are sometimes criticized by readers of the book. E. M. Halliday, for example, remarks: "One is likely to feel not so much that Frederic Henry thought these thoughts at the time, as that Frederic Henry—or Ernest Hemingway—thought them retrospectively, and is delivering short lectures with his eyes on the audience rather than on the story itself." This bothers Halliday as a "thematic intrusion," this occasional habit of interruption to insist that glorious rhetoric is phony and that good people get destroyed.[11] Hemingway has not, of course, written a flawless book, but it does seem that the "thematic" passages are easily justified and quite organic. They are indeed "retrospective"; they are the lieutenant's thoughts as he is writing the book, as he is clumsily grasping (quite understandably) for some strands of philosophy after all that he has experienced.[12] Here Halliday is right. But are Henry's (or Hemingway's) "eyes on the audience"? Henry's eyes, which are the eyes we are mainly interested in, seem rather to be gazing nervously on the senseless and tragic world—on the main part of his world which has stopped, stopped for no good reason whatsoever, except as the anonymous Fates inscrutably dictate. They are eyes that feebly try to perceive a principle—"Stay around and they would kill you" (338). This is because sanity demands some sort of organizing principle. That explains where Henry's eyes are; we need not be in a hurry to fault the book on that ground when a plausible reason lies before us.

There is one recapitulation to be made as we cease analysis and put the book back together for an overview. If we are to let this book reach us, to let this one man's closed history touch us, we must be prepared to relinquish finally our impulse to be scientists, biographers, and theologians. As scientists we can state that a man named Hemingway has made this book at a given time, has invented a man named Henry, and in a number of particulars has done this and not that. As biographers we find the "code," the restraint, the drinking, the reticence, to be part of an attempted salvation pattern. Frederic Henry is one apostle in the canon, and the Hemingway religion is founded on the gospels of Jake, Nick,

---

[11] "Hemingway's Narrative Perspective," *Sewanee Review,* LX (Spring, 1952), 211.
[12] It is true, however, that he says of his disgust with war rhetoric, "I was *always* embarrassed" (191).

Frederic and the Pauline subtlists of the academy. But in asking why the book is what it is, why so much is left out, why the mood is so severe, the prose so spare, the picture of Catherine and her lover so fragile, we do well to become as children and act as if Frederic Henry had signed his name to the story. If we can believe this—if we can believe in Frederic Henry—we are in the place Hemingway wants us to be. And this place is a vantage point for observing certain precise boundaries that have been constructed for our scrutiny. From this vantage point we will see framed at a just distance and with the right degree of dark clarity the three portions of Frederic Henry's world that have stopped, that are momentarily in focus before receding from him and now also from us.

Daniel J. Schneider

Hemingway's *A Farewell to Arms:* The Novel as Pure Poetry

In a well-known essay[1] Robert Penn Warren has drawn a distinction between two kinds of poetry, a "pure" poetry, which seeks more or less systematically to exclude so-called "unpoetic" elements from its hushed and hypnotic atmosphere, and an "impure," a poetry of inclusion or synthesis, which welcomes into itself such supposedly recalcitrant and inhospitable stuff as wit, cacophony, jagged rhythms, and intellectual debate. The distinction between the two types, so helpful in the analysis of lyrics, may obviously be employed to advantage in the criticism of novels, and I should like to use it here to call attention to an aspect of Hemingway's art that has not received any extended comment. For if there are works, such as *War and Peace, Ulysses, Moby Dick,* and *The Magic Mountain,* whose power and beauty are best explained by their very "impurity"—novels that batten on the diversity of life and are most themselves when they are most "loose and baggy" (to use James's fine phrase)—the strength of

Reprinted from *Modern Fiction Studies,* XIV (Autumn, 1968), 283-296.
Reprinted by permission of the author and *Modern Fiction Studies,* © 1969, by Purdue Research Foundation, Lafayette, Indiana.
[1] "Pure and Impure Poetry," *Selected Essays* (New York, 1957).

Hemingway's novels is explained best, I think, by noting that they are in spirit and in method closer to pure lyric than to epic, and that they systematically exclude whatever threatens to interfere with the illusion of life beheld under the aspect of a single, dominant, all-pervasive mood or state of mind. They attempt to sustain perfectly a single emotion: they begin with it and end with it, and any scenes, characters, thoughts, or stylistic elements that might tend to weaken the dominant emotion are ruthlessly rejected. Consequently, Hemingway's art has both the virtues and the limitations of lyricism: maximum intensity on the one hand, extremely limited range on the other.

/ Hemingway's *A Farewell to Arms* is I think one of the purest lyric novels ever written./But if we are fully to appreciate its power—and the power of a number of other works by Hemingway —we are driven to examine the poetics of this lyricism[2] and to assess, if we can, the extent to which Hemingway has exploited the possibilities of the type.

I

The dominant emotion or state of mind behind the events of *A Farewell to Arms* is seldom stated explicitly. It is always there, informing every scene of the novel, lying beneath every descriptive passage and every bit of characterization, but it seldom shows, or it shows, at most, but a tiny part of itself, like the iceberg that Hemingway often took to be the apt image of his art. It is a bitterness, a disgust, a desolation of soul, a remorse of such depth and durance that it can be held in check only by dint of the severest, most unremitting self-control. When it does show itself clearly, this inner violence, as in Chapter XXXIV of *Farewell*, it is expressed in this way:

> If people bring so much courage to this world the world has to kill them to break them, so of course it kills them. The world breaks every one and afterward many are strong at the broken places. But those that will not break it kills. It kills the very good and the very gentle and the very brave impartially. If you are none of these you can be sure it will kill you too but there will be no special hurry.[3]

---

[2] For a sensitive analysis of the characteristics and possibilities of the lyric novel see Ralph Freedman, *The Lyrical Novel* (Princeton, 1963), Chapters 1, 2, and 6.

[3] New York: Scribner Library, p. 249. Hereafter page references will be given in the text.

The world's malevolence is taken for granted in Hemingway's novels. The artistic problem Hemingway faced was to find the correlatives of his bitterness—objects adequate to the emotion, techniques capable of rendering it as purely as possible. The tragic action, involving failure, humiliation, and, especially, the punishment and defeat of lovers was of course the chief means of conveying the essential vision, the essential bitterness. But a whole poetics of the novel which confines itself to the embodiment of such a state of mind had to be developed, and it is in the solution of minor as well as of major problems that the genius of Hemingway is finally revealed. His style, for example—the perfect correlative (as Brooks and Warren have shown) of his sense of the ruthless and arbitrary condition of the world that breaks and kills—becomes the perfect correlative too of the emotions of despair and bitterness. The careful selection of a dominant image and its reiteration through whole paragraphs and pages and chapters, so that the image presently becomes symbol, conveying both the central meaning and the central emotion, becomes Hemingway's fixed method. Perhaps the best analogy is found in the choice of a musical key and in the elaborate harmonization of notes always referring to the tonic. Ideally, when the writing is purest, every sentence will bespeak the central meaning and emotion. There will be no purely functional passages, no passages which merely illustrate a meaning, no characters or episodes given freedom to develop emotions outside the dominant bitterness. Everything will be converted into a symbol of the emotion. Where such conversion does not take place, the art fails and the novel becomes epic, not lyric; narrative, instead of the pure utterance of passion.

The determination to make the novel lyrical inevitably influences all of its parts. Character becomes, in one sense, unimportant. Characters exist for the sake of the emotion and, as in most lyric poems, need not be three-dimensional. Indeed, any full and vivid particularization of character is likely to work against the dominant emotion, for when a character is complex and fully realized, he is scarcely able to maintain a single, fixed emotion or state of mind. It is only rather highly generalized characters who can feel "purely." A lovely and brave young woman may function well in a lyric world. Represent her in such complicated terms as Joyce employs to depict Leopold Bloom and the emotion is adulterated by a thousand reservations and ironic complexities. Of course character cannot be *reduced* to passion: a writer like Poe frequently fails because he is so much interested in feeling that he virtually eliminates character altogether; but Poe's Gothic tales suggest the proper direction of the lyric novel: character must exist for the sake of the emotion, and wherever the variety and diversity of life threaten to dilute or dissipate the central emotion, life must be excluded from the novel. It is thus no fair criticism to say that Hemingway has created no memorable characters; the truth is that his novels necessarily reject such people. One may imagine what Hemingway would have to do with the "memorable" Buck Mulligan to adjust him to the world of *Farewell*. Much of the elan of the Joycean character would necessarily be sacrificed to the mood of the scene, and only so much of Mulligan's irreverence as would not undermine the sense of despair would be recorded. In short, what is rolicking insouciance in Joyce would become, in Hemingway, the doleful chant of "irony and pity"; the Rabelaisian humor would be infused with the central bitterness, and would scarcely be humor at all: Mulligan would become Rinaldi.

The action, too, must obviously become, as nearly as possible, simple, intellectually uncomplicated, and, in spirit if not in actual construction, akin to lyric soliloquy. An action involving much intellectual debate, analysis, repartee, or a multiplication of points of view is clearly antithetical to the spirit of Hemingway's lyric novels. For cerebration tends to destroy passion; intellectual analysis or agility introduces a note of objectivity that the lyric novel cannot tolerate, and debate might require the introduction of spokesmen whose personalities and whose mere presence could shatter the lyric mood. It is for this reason that the action of Hemingway's lyric novels approaches, whenever it can, the scene of prolonged suffering. The characteristic sources of complication are not new complications of "plot" in the sense that fresh *problems* are introduced to be debated and solved, but rather new wounds, new torments, so that bitterness deepens and grows toward a pitch of anguish and remorse. Hemingway is always reluctant to introduce actions that do not feed the dominant emotion (sometmes so close to self-pity) and in consequence his characteristic way of structuring the action of his novels is to employ a simple qualitative shift or oscillation between despair and happiness. In *The Sun Also Rises* the shifts are from Paris, to Burguete, to Pamplona, to San Sebastian; in *A Farewell to Arms* they are from the front, to the hospital, to the front, to Switzerland; disgust and bitterness, followed by a short respite, then back to disgust and bitterness again. The dominant emotion is intensified through these powerful contrasts with opposite emotions. And major form is reinforced by minor: brief scenes in which characters are represented as enjoying intensely food and drink or a lovely view or a simple physical comfort exist chiefly to heighten the sense of despair and bitterness; the interludes of normal pleasure are inevitably shortlived; by various signs we know that they will soon be over and that whatever one has will be taken away. Every meal, every sight, every sound thus comes to one as to a man about to be executed. That is one reason the descriptions of food and drink always seem so preternaturally vivid in Hemingway.

It is unnecessary to extend this poetics further at this point. We shall see, if we look closely at *A Farewell to Arms*, how thoroughly Hemingway has exploited the possibilities of his lyric form.

II

In *A Farewell to Arms* the dominant state of mind—the sense of death, defeat, failure, nothingness, emptiness—is conveyed chiefly by the image of the rain (with all its tonal associates, *mist, wet, damp, river, fog*), by images and epithets of desolation (chiefly *bare, thin, small,* and *fallen leaves*), and by images and epithets of impurity and corruption (chiefly *dust, mud, dirt,* and *disease*). Hemingway's method of working with the images is surprisingly uniform. I have already employed an analogy of music; another way of describing the method is to think of a painter working tiny patches of a dominant color over his entire canvas. Hemingway himself perhaps had both analogies in mind when he said, in the Lillian Ross interview, that he had "learned how to make a landscape from Mr. Paul Cezanne" and mentioned, in the same context, his imitation of Bach's counterpoint in the first chapter of *Farewell*.[4] The images are repeated so frequently that they begin to toll like bells in the mind. Virtually every sentence says, "Death, despair, failure, emptiness," because virtually every sentence contains an image or symbol associated with the dominant state of mind.

The novel begins with this state of mind, and it is established so firmly, through the repetition of the central symbols, that any emotions other than bitterness and despair may thereafter intrude

[4] "How Do You Like It Now, Gentlemen?" in *Hemingway: A Collection of Critical Essays,* ed. Robert P. Weeks (Englewood Cliffs, N.J., 1962), p. 36.

only with difficulty. The typical procedure, as in lyric poetry, is to intensify the dominant emotion by means of a simple contrast of images. Thus the images of purity and vitality, introduced in the second sentence of the novel, are contrasted throughout the chapter with the images of dirt and failure:

> In the late summer of that year we lived in a house in a village that looked across the river and the plain to the mountains. In the bed of the river there were pebbles and boulders, dry and white in the sun, and the water was clear and swiftly moving and blue in the channels. Troops went by the house and down the road and the dust they raised powdered the leaves of the trees. The trunks of the trees too were dusty and the leaves fell early that year and we saw the troops marching along the road and the dust rising and leaves, stirred by the breeze, falling and the soldiers marching and afterward the road bare and white except for the leaves. (p. 3)

Purity has been defiled, the life-force has been thwarted and defeated. The leaves are "powdered" by dust; the trunks too are "dusty"; the leaves fall "early"; and the empty road, "bare and white except for the leaves," becomes a perfect correlative of the inner desolation. The defilement and violation of life is further suggested by a reference to camouflage ("There were big guns that passed in the day drawn by tractors, the long barrels of the guns covered with green branches and green leafy branches and vines laid over the tractor" [p. 4]) and by a reference to the cartridge-boxes bulging under the capes of the soldiers "so that the men, passing on the road, marched as though they were six months gone with child" (p. 4). And these bitter ironies are reinforced by the introduction of the dominant symbol of the rain: not life-giving rain causing the leaves to grow but the autumnal and winter rain causing them to fall, a rain associated with darkness, mud, and death:

> There was fighting for that mountain too, but it was not successful, and in the fall when the rains came the leaves all fell from the chestnut trees and the branches were bare and the trunks were black with rain. The vineyards were thin and bare-branched too and all the country wet and brown and dead with the autumn. There were mists over the river and clouds on the mountain and the trucks splashed mud on the road and the troops were muddy and wet in their capes; their rifles were wet. . . . (p. 4)

The sense of failure and impotence is also reinforced by the studious avoidance of action-verbs. Almost invariably Hemingway employs the copulative *to be*, and the expletives *there were* and *there was* occur ten times in the twenty-one sentences of the chapter, six of the sentences being introduced by them. The repetitions give a sense of endless sameness and weariness: abandon hope, all ye who enter here.

The concluding paragraphs of the chapter reinforce what has already been established powerfully. The guns, the tractors, the motor-cars show a ruthless power, and it is as if life, in the presence of these overwhelming forces of death, had withered and shrunk. The "very small" king, sitting in the speeding motor-car "between two generals," becomes a fine correlative of the sense of impotence:

> There were small gray motor cars that passed going very fast; usually there was an officer in the seat with the driver and more officers in the back seat. They splashed more mud than the camions even and if one of the officers in the back was very small and sitting between two generals, he himself so small that you could not see his face but only the top of his cap and his narrow back, and if the car went especially fast it was probably the king. He lived in Udine and came out in this way nearly every day to see how things were going, and things went very badly.
>
> At the start of the winter came the permanent rain and with the rain came the cholera. But it was checked and in the end only seven thousand died of it in the army. (p. 4)

With this last paragraph the sense of doom is complete. The rain is "permanent" and the apparent consolation, the fact that the cholera is checked, is viciously undercut by the irony that "*only* seven thousand died of it in the army."

The mood of the first chapter is thus established powerfully through the proliferation of associated images, images written in a single key. But to continue in this way—that is, to continue to present events and people as the objectification of feeling through the modulation of images—would of course be to drive narrative out of the novel; there would be no "story," only bitterness distilled. Hemingway's artistic problem accordingly becomes that of presenting action and conflict in such a way that the central emotion will not be shattered by the inclusion of elements hostile to it. As I have indicated, action must be converted into passion; characters must become embodiments of the central bitterness.

When it becomes necessary, then, in Chapter II, to introduce characters and to develop a scene whose essential quality is potentially uncongenial to the established emotion, Hemingway must take pains to weaken or nullify the inharmonious effects and to absorb character and scene into the dominant mood. So it is that when the priest, the captain, and the other soldiers are introduced, Hemingway guards against any dilution of the central emotion by framing the scene with a description expressive, once again, of the profound regret and bitterness:

> Later, below in the town, I watched the snow falling, looking out of the window of the bawdy house, the house for officers, where I sat with a friend and two glasses drinking a bottle of Asti, and, looking out at the snow falling slowly and heavily, we knew it was all over for that year. Up the river the mountains had not been taken; none of the mountains beyond the river had been taken. That was all left for next year. My friend saw the priest from our mess going by in the street, walking carefully in the slush, and pounded on the window to attract his attention. The priest looked up. He saw us and smiled. My friend motioned for him to come in. The priest shook his head and went on. That night in the mess after the spaghetti course . . . the captain commenced picking on the priest. (pp. 6-7)

In the scene that follows, the captain's baiting of the priest takes its tone from the frame and is anything but humorous. The "good fun" is swallowed up by the pervasive sadness and bitterness, and the episode acts upon the reader in much the same way as an episode in *The Waste Land* affects Eliot's readers: dialogue, narrative, description are all viewed as expressions of the central fears and desires. The characters introduced are not important in themselves; their development as characters does not interest the writer. They are aspects of the hero's state of mind, and represent, covertly, the conflicts of his soul.

We must note, moreover, that the scene is, characteristically, short. For to lengthen any scene of this sort, in which the actions and speeches of minor characters threaten to shake our awareness of the hero's mood, would be fatal to the lyric novel. If developed at length, the scene would cease to function as the token of the hero's feelings. E. M. Forster, in his *Aspects of the Novel*, has pointed out the danger of the characters' taking the story out of the novelist's control. The minor characters, if freed from the hero's sensibility, would take the scene into their own hands. The rhythm and mood of the scene would be theirs, not the hero's, and the scene, instead of reinforcing, might easily weaken or dissipate the central emotion. Furthermore, any particularly vivid rendering of the inherent "coloring" of the events and speeches— such rendering as one finds everywhere in the novels of Dickens —might work dangerously against the emotion. Hence the scene must be reported as barely, as "objectively" as possible. Perhaps it has not been sufficiently appreciated that "objectivity," as employed by Hemingway, is more than a means of effective understatement or of being true to the facts; it is also, much of the time, a means of preventing alien attitudes and feelings from asserting themselves vigorously—at the expense of the dominant emotion of the lyric novel. Of course objectivity *also* gives an air of distance and detachment; but where the objectively rendered scene is framed by lyric passages of great intensity, the scene becomes suffused with the emotion of the antecedent lyric, and it is precisely the deadpan reporting with the recurrent "he saids" that *permits* such penetration of the emotion.

The depression of Frederic Henry continues into Chapter III, but by this time the impressions of bitterness and failure have accumulated so densely that one is ready for a shift to an opposite state of mind. Returning from his leave, Frederic finds everything at the front unchanged. He has not gone to Abruzzi, as the priest urged him to, and, as the symbolism suggests delicately, he is mired in moral filth and inertia. Rinaldi, after kissing him, says: "You're dirty. . . . You ought to wash," and in Chapter IV Frederic observes, "I was very dusty and dirty and went up to my room to wash" (p. 17). In truth he needs a kind of purification. Thus when he sees Catherine Barkley for the first time in the garden of the British hospital, the imagery hints at the purity, the Eden-like peace that Frederic most deeply craves: "Miss Barkley was in the garden. Another nurse was with her. We saw their white uniforms through the trees and walked toward them" (p. 18). But the first conversation of the lovers, with its truncated, tight-lipped exchanges, only reiterates the desperation and despair that have already pervaded the novel. Once a key word has been sounded, Hemingway modulates it beautifully in half a dozen different shadings, until the conversation, like the descriptions already quoted, becomes a refrain on the theme of failure:

> "Yes," she said. "People can't realize what France is like. If they did, it couldn't go on. He didn't have a sabre cut. They blew him all to bits."

I didn't say anything.
"Do you suppose it will always go on?"
"No."
"What's to stop it?"
"It will crack somewhere."
"We'll crack. We'll crack in France. They can't go on doing
things like the Somme and not crack."
"They won't crack here," I said.
"You think not?"
"No. They did very well last summer."
"They may crack," she said. "Anybody may crack."
"The Germans too."
"No," she said. "I think not." (p. 20)

Catherine here exists almost as the echo of Frederic's own bitterness and despair. She is Despair turning desperately to the religion
of love. She has no past beyond the absolute minimum required
for plausibility. Like another Catherine, Bronte's Catherine Earn-
shaw, she *is* her lover: her temperamental affinity to Frederic is so
marked that their right to each other is accepted almost from the
first moment of meeting. Thus she is, in a sense, not a distinct
character at all but Frederic's bitterness or his desire objectified.
She will presently become the peace or bliss that stands at farthest
remove from the war: the white snows of the mountaintops, the
idyllic serenity of Switzerland, the Beatrice of the *Paradiso*. To
lose her will be to lose Love. The lyric novel requires no deeper
characterization.

Once she has been introduced, Hemingway is ready to effect the
first qualitative shift in the novel. He has only to bring about the
circumstances that will make possible a brief interlude of love and
joy—a state of mind opposite to the intolerable mood of the opening chapters. In Chapter VII Frederic returns to the front, and
the sweat, the heat, and the dust are again emphasized (p. 33).
References to washing or taking baths recur (pp. 36, 39), and in
Chapter IX, when he is wounded, we are told that so much dirt
has blown into the wound that it has not hemorrhaged much (p.
57). The form of the next several chapters, then, becomes the
gradual emergence from the filth and darkness of the war into the
purity and light of love. The slow healing of Frederic's wound is
concomitant with a subtle, incomplete healing of his soul, and
before his return to the front he will have acquired, though without fully knowing it, the conviction that neither Rinaldi, who visits
him in Chapter X, nor the priest, who visits him in Chapter
XI, can claim his soul: his love of Catherine is his religion.

Yet this first idyll of love is by no means as pure and satisfying as the second interlude in Switzerland. It alters Frederic's disposition; it teaches him that love is possible; but it does not bring such full and radiant joy as will come later. It must, of necessity, be less complete, less satisfying, than the Switzerland episodes; if it were not, the happiness in Switzerland would be anti-climactic, and there would be no conviction that the lovers had grown emotionally and spiritually in such a way as to make the shattering of their union fully tragic. At this stage of the action Hemingway therefore wisely presents only so much of the lovers' joy as will establish a strong contrast between the old state of mind and the new. The moments of joy are intermittent. There are still, even after Frederic's recovery, many ominous suggestions of the old hollowness and despair. The ugliness of Ettore's ambition to rise and win glory in the army reminds the lovers of the world they want to forget. The rain returns and Catherine, who sometimes sees herself "dead in it," is frightened and begins to cry; in Chapter XX the dishonesty of the fixed horse-races sullies the lovers' afternoon, though they are able to outwit the world by betting on a horse they've never heard of (named symbolically "Light for Me") and Catherine says, "I feel so much cleaner." But in Chapter XXI Catherine announces that she is pregnant, and the uncertainty of the future stirs a new dread. In the next chapter the rain returns: "It turned cold that night and the next day it was raining. Coming home from the Ospedale Maggiore it rained very hard and I was wet when I came in. Up in my room the rain was coming down heavily outside on the balcony, and the wind blew it against the glass doors" (p. 142). Frederic comes down with jaundice, a physical correlative of the old sense of "rottenness," and the visit he and Catherine had planned to Pallanza is now out of the question. The old pattern of failure reasserts itself. When Miss Van Campen discovers the empty bottles in the armoire of his hospital room, his leave is cancelled.

In Chapter XXIII, the night on which Frederic returns to the front, the rain, the lovers' goodbyes, and the sense of helplessness all combine to produce a profound pathos and anguish that passes, finally, into a bitterness even more intense than that of the opening chapters. The chapter begins with Frederic's making arrangements to have a seat on the troop train held for him and with his saying goodbye at the hospital. The wife of the porter weeps. Frederic walks to a wine-shop and waits for Catherine to pass. At this point the rain of despair and death is suggested only by mist and fog: "It was dark outside and cold and misty. . . . There was a fog in the square and when we came close to the front of the cathedral it was very big and the stone was wet" (pp. 146-147). Frederic asks Catherine if she would like to go in, but she says no, and they go instead to a hotel where the furniture of vice, red plush curtains, a satin coverlet on the bed, and "many mirrors," besmirch the sacredness of their love. On their trip to the hotel the fog changes to rain, and the sense of failure and loss deepens:

> "We can get a cab at the bridge," I said. We stood on the bridge *in the fog* waiting for a carriage. Several streetcars passed, full of people going home. Then a carriage came along but there was someone in it. *The fog was turning to rain.*
> "We could walk or take a train," Catherine said.
> "One will be along," I said. "They go by here.
> "Here one comes," she said.
> The driver stopped his horse and lowered the metal sign on his meter. The top of the carriage was up and there were *drops of water* on the driver's coat. His varnished hat was *shining in the wet.* We sat back in the seat together and the top of the carriage made it dark. (p. 150; italics mine)

In the hotel Catherine bursts out: "I never felt like a whore before." Frederic stands at the window looking down at "the wet pavement" until Catherine calls him back to the bed. For a time the lovers are happy in the hotel room, which, in a bitter irony, Catherine refers to as their "fine house" and their "home." But in a moment of stillness they can "hear the rain" (p. 154) and presently they must leave. The symbolic rain now finds its way into almost every sentence, as if doom were complete, inescapable:

> I saw the carriage coming. It stopped, the horse's head hanging *in the rain,* and the waiter stepped out, *opened his umbrella,* and came toward the hotel. We met him at the door and walked out *under the umbrella* down *the wet walk* to the carriage at the curb. *Water was running in the gutter.*
> "There is your package on the seat," the waiter said. He stood *with the umbrella* until we were in and I had tipped him.
> "Many thanks. Pleasant journey," he said. The coachman lifted the reins and the horse started. The waiter turned away *under the umbrella* and went toward the hotel. We drove down the street and turned to the left, then came around to the right in front of the station. There were two carabinieri standing under the light just *out of the rain.* The light shone on their hats. *The*

rain was clear and transparent against the light from the station. A porter came out from under the shelter of the station, his shoulders up *against the rain.* (p. 157; italics mine)

When Frederic enters the crowded troop-train, where "every one was hostile," the return to the old bitterness is virtually complete. He gives up his seat to the belligerent captain with the "new and shiny" scar, then stands watching the lights of the station as the train pulls out. Light has been associated from the beginning with Catherine, her white uniform and, especially, her shining hair (p. 114). Just before boarding the train, Frederic sees her face "in the light" (p. 157). But now "It was still raining and soon the windows were wet and you could not see out" (p. 159). The violence of the shift from the interlude of love to the nightmare of the war is consummately rendered in the final sentences of the chapter: Frederic is swallowed up in a hell of darkness, congestion, and hostility, and the loss of his identity as lover is complete; he sleeps on the floor of the corridor, thinking: "they could all walk over me if they wouldn't step on me. Men were sleeping on the floor all down the corridor. Others stood holding on to the window rods or leaning against the doors. That train was always crowded" (p. 159).

The world has again triumphed. Accordingly, the sense of desolation and failure at the beginning of Book Three is almost identical with that of the novel's first chapter. Once again it is autumn, and once again Hemingway uses the limited palette of key words to paint the emotion, building his opening paragraph on the adjective "bare" and on references to the rain and to "shrunken" life:

> Now in the fall the trees were all *bare* and the roads were muddy. I rode to Gorizia from Udine on a camion. We passed other camions on the road and I looked at the country. The mulberry trees were *bare* and the fields were brown. There were *wet* dead leaves on the road from the rows of *bare* trees and men were working on the road, tamping stone in the ruts from piles of crushed stone along the side of the road between the trees. We saw the town *with a mist over it* that cut off the mountains. We crossed the river and I saw that it was running high. *It had been raining* in the mountains. We came into the town past the factories and then the houses and villas and I saw many more houses had been hit. On a narrow street we passed a British Red Cross ambulance. The driver wore a cap and his face was *thin* and very tanned. I did not know him. I got down from the camion in the

big square in front of the Town Major's house, the driver handed down my rucksack and I put it on and swung on the two musettes and walked to our villa. It did not feel like a homecoming.

I walked down the *damp* gravel driveway looking at the villa through the trees. The windows were all shut but the door was open. I went in and found the major sitting at a table in the *bare* room with maps and typed sheets of paper on the wall. (pp. 163-164; italics mine)

The old sense of pollution also returns: Rinaldi, who fears he has syphilis, chides Frederic for trying to cleanse his conscience with a toothbrush. And the sense of impotence and failure is further objectified in Rinaldi's "You can't do it. You can't do it. I say you can't do it. You're dry and you're empty and there's nothing else. There's nothing else I tell you" (p. 174). Presently Frederic picks up the refrain: he believes "in sleep," he tells the priest, "meaning nothing" (p. 179). Then in Chapter XXVII the rains begin again:

It stormed all that day. The wind drove down *the rain* and everywhere there was *standing water* and mud. The plaster of the broken houses was gray and *wet*. Late in the afternoon *the rain* stopped and from out number two post I saw the *bare wet* autumn country with clouds over the tops of the hills and the straw screening over the road *wet and dripping*. The sun came out once before it went down and shone on the *bare* woods beyond the ridge. . . . We loaded two cars and drove down the road that was screened with *wet* mats and the last of the sun came through in the breaks between the strips of matting. Before we were out on the clear road behind the hill the sun was down. We went on down the clear road and as it turned into the open and went into the square arched tunnel of matting *the rain started again*.

The wind rose in the night and at three o'clock in the morning *with the rain coming in sheets* there was a bombardment and the Croatians came over across the mountain meadows and through the patches of wood and into the front line. They fought *in the dark in the rain* and a counter-attack of scared men from the second line drove them back. There was much shelling and many rockets *in the rain* and machine-gun and rifle fire all along the line. They did not come again and it was quieter and between *the gusts of wind and rain* we could hear the sound of a great bombardment far to the north. (pp. 185-186; italics mine)

The retreat begins, "orderly, wet and sullen," with troops marching "under the rain" (p. 188). In Chapter XXVII the word "rain" appears twenty-four times; in Chapter XXVIII, seventeen times. Chapter XXVII begins with a reference to sleep—meaning, of course, nothing—and in twelve pages the word appears, incredibly, as noun, adjective, or verb, thirty-three times. I am aware that such counting is not in itself a proof of the lyric progression of these events, but when rain means death and sleep means nothing, the recurrence of the words builds a mood of absolute hopelessness.

Moreover, because of the repetitions, a note of desperation comes to suffuse the scene: the pressure of the accumulated bitterness will become too intense, and the dominant emotion will again seek to elicit its opposite, pure peace, pure happiness, the pure joy of love. After the overwhelming development of the emotion in these chapters, Frederic's bolt for freedom cannot be far off. Hemingway can sustain the emotion for a few chapters more, but any further prolongation would make the intensity commonplace and the evil banal, meaningless. Frederic must soon fall into the hands of the battle-police. A very brief qualitative shift in Chapter XXX enables Hemingway to prolong the suffering for an additional chapter: the interlude in the barn depicts a normality, a wholesomeness and sanity that appear with great force after the nightmare of the retreat ("The hay smelled good and lying in the hay took away all the years in between. We had lain in hay and talked and shot sparrows with an air-rifle when they perched in the triangle cut high up in the wall of the barn" [p. 216]), but the war is too close, the barn provides only momentary respite, and Frederic must quickly move out into the "black night with the rain." The scene in which he confronts the battle-police occurs within four pages after the departure from the barn.

Once Frederic has fled, the lyric form of the novel is predictable: the interlude in Switzerland followed by the crushing failure in the hospital. Once again the rhythm of the novel becomes that of emergence from darkness and failure. The rain continues as Frederic crosses the symbolic Venetian plain (Chapter XXXI), as he takes the train to Stresa, and as he and Catherine lie in the hotel room there (Chapter XXXIV). In Chapter XXXV there occurs a brief interlude of sanity and peace in which Frederic trolls for lake trout with the barman and plays billiards with Count Greffi; but Chapter XXXVI begins: "That night there was a storm and I woke to hear the rain lashing the window-panes" (p. 264), and in "the dark and the rain" (p. 266) Frederic and Catherine set out for Switzerland. In Chapter XXXVII Frederic rows all night as the rain comes "occasionally in gusts" (p. 270). But when they set foot in Switzerland a second and more perfect idyll of love and purity commences.

Here again, as in the earlier interlude, Hemingway wisely guards against sentimentalizing the period of happiness. The religion of love is not enough: there is anxiety about the future, and Catherine is quick to notice that Frederic is chafing because he has nothing to do. But after the prolonged suffering and failure of the middle section of the novel, the impression of perfect joy is very strong, and the emotion is objectified in dozens of images suggesting sanity, wholesomeness, purity, and peace. Energy returns: "it was good walking on the road and invigorating" (p. 290). The snow on the mountain peaks, like the snows of Kilimanjaro, is a correlative of the sense of heavenly bliss and purity. The sun shines, and the air is "cold and clear" (p. 291). By January the winter settles into "bright cold days and hard cold nights." The snow is now "clean packed" (p. 303); the air comes "sharply into your lungs"; there is now a sense that the life-force has *not* been defeated, and the lovers see foxes; the night is "dry and cold and very clear" (p. 304).

It is not until March, when the winter breaks (Chapter XL) and it begins raining that the old failure and bitterness threaten to shatter the lovers' happiness. Then, in the magnificent last chapter, the pattern of failure is sharply reasserted in a terrible echo of Rinaldi's "You can't do it." All of Catherine's efforts to give birth to the child fail. She cries out that the anesthetic is "not working." The child is strangled by the umbilical cord; the Caesarian fails. Even Frederic's effort to say good-by fails: "It wasn't any good. It was like saying good-by to a statue" (p. 332). And so he is delivered up, once again, to the rain of death and failure: "After a while I went out and left the hospital and walked back to the hotel in the rain." The two attempts to escape the world's malice have failed, just as, in *The Sun Also Rises*, the two interludes of sanity and purity (the trout-fishing episode and the swimming episode at San Sebastian) provide only brief respite from the world; and one is left with the conviction that any further effort to escape will be crushed with equal ruthlessness.

The basic rhythm of the action of *Farewell* is thus almost identical with that of Hemingway's earlier novel, and the symbolism, too, is virtually unchanged. It seems safe to say that Hemingway had established his art in his earlier book: he had learned that lyricism was his essential talent, and he set about deliberately to apply the knowledge imparted by the earlier lessons. Over the next thirty years he was not to make any significant changes in his basic method. If there was a slight decline in his creative energy in the later books, if some of them seem mechanical, their style having become self-conscious mannerism rather than the perfect objectification of lyric impulses, the defects were scarcely so great as to impair the central vitality of his work. For he had developed his lyric art with the utmost attention to every means of rendering emotion purely. By 1929 he knew so well what he could do and how he could do it that he had reduced the possibilities of failure to a minimum. To adventure into the epic novel might have proved disastrous to an artist of Hemingway's limited powers. Provided that he confined himself to the lyric art he knew so thoroughly, he was not likely to fail. It is perhaps no small part of his genius that he seems to have recognized his limitations and to have made maximum use of the materials available to his lyric sensibility.

Blanche Gelfant

Language as a Moral Code in
A Farewell to Arms

For the novelist, the danger of the cliché is not merely staleness of language; it is dullr   ʿ ⁻ᵃ⁻ᵖᵗⁱᵒⁿ—and dullness has both esthetic and moral imⲣ   Ernest Hemingway who held purity of lan   andard pursued clarity of vision as his r   r such a writer the relationship between   word was of utmost concern. It was a r   ⟨o remain completely reciprocal: the exper   ⟨e word, and the word in turn was to recall   eciprocity is destroyed by the cliché. The   ⟨xperiences into stereotyped patterns of ⲣ   ⟩n, patterns which cannot recreate accuraᵗ   ⟨cause they do not evoke the unique and mⲟ   ⟨ experience. The cliché makes invidious use of the ⲣⲟⲣ.   ⟩rds to escape from the encounter with truth. The use of the cliché as one's idiom implies

---

Reprinted from *Modern Fiction Studies,* IX (1963), 173-176. Reprinted by permission of the author and *Modern Fiction Studies,* © 1969, by Purdue Research Foundation, Lafayette, Indiana.
¹ See Carlos Baker, *Hemingway: The Writer as Artist* (Princeton University Press, 1956 ed.), pp. 48 ff..

then a kind of moral capitulation, a willingness to settle for less than truth or clarity of vision and a willingness to embrace words for the comfort of their familiarity. Thus staleness of language may reflect obtuseness or evasiveness and sometimes even fear.

It is fear that leads Frederic Henry in a crucial scene in *A Farewell to Arms*[2] to fall back on the ever-ready cliché despite his earlier impassioned denunciation of its uses in war[3] and his consistent avoidance of it in all circumstances. Frederic's brief interior monologue on the possibility of Catherine's death is interesting stylistically because Hemingway seems here to forsake the ideal of purity of expression and to rely instead upon mere banalities. The language is trite and repetitious to the point of compulsion; the sentences are distressingly simple; and the movement is erratic, syncopated by the nervous rushes and ebbs of fear. But closer study of the monologue reveals the marvelous economy of Hemingway's art as well as a highly creative use of the cliché. Through the very banalities of the passage, the repetitions, the erratic tempo and dialectic structure, Hemingway expresses simultaneously several levels of experience—Frederic's surface panic and the scurry of his immediate thoughts, the underlying depths of his anxiety, and the total moral integrity of his character.

As the monologue allows Frederic to verbalize his fears, it shows him undergoing the crucial test of the Hemingway hero. Like the young man in initiation, or the bullfighter, hunter, soldier, or prizefighter, Frederic is confronting the fact of death and so taking measure of his courage. Frederic's courage consists in the willingness to face reality. In all situations he has rejected the ready clichés with which men immure themselves in illusions, whether those of love, war, or sacrifice. For Frederic, as for most Hemingway heroes, the inescapable reality of life is death.[4] Death is "the end of the trap." Now the trap has been sprung to catch Catherine, and Frederic, having staked his happiness on Catherine, is caught along with her. He knows that they are trapped, but he

---

[2] Ernest Hemingway, *A Farewell to Arms* (Scribner's Modern Standard Authors, 1957 ed.), pp. 330-331.

[3] *A Farewell to Arms*, p. 191. This is the famous and much-quoted passage which begins, "I was always embarrassed by the words sacred, glorious, sacrifice and the expression in vain. . . ." Frederic's point here is specifically that such abstract words have no relation to the actual deeds of war; they are meaningless, even "obscene."

[4] See James F. Light, "The Religion of Death in *A Farewell to Arms*," *Modern Fiction Studies* VII (1961), 169-173.

knows also that the only courageous gesture is to try to escape. Hence the passage expresses the excruciating tension of the struggle against all odds, a struggle which takes place in Frederic's mind as he returns at least ten times to the question of death in his thrashing effort to evade the inevitable. As Frederic's thoughts race back and forth from the possibility of death to denial, the movement of the passage simulates the scurrying movement of the trapped creature in a maze. Frederic's unexpressed fear that there is no way out of the maze—that death cannot be denied— leads him to the round of hackneyed but possibly reassuring expressions called forth in such moments of stress. "A bad time," "protracted initial labor," "just nature"—are these not the set phrases suitable to such an occasion?; have they not been suggested by doctor and nurse?; and should not Frederic at least try them all? Women in labor have "a bad time"; men always pace the floor. Frederic creates out of a few pat phrases a kind of incantation, as though repetition of words can exorcise the fact of death.

> She's just having a bad time. The initial labor is usually protracted. She's only having a bad time. Afterward we'd say what a bad time and Catherine would say it wasn't really so bad. But what if she should die? She can't die. Yes, but what if she should die? She can't, I tell you. Don't be a fool. It's just a bad time. It's just nature giving her hell. It's only the first labor, which is almost always protracted. (p. 331)

Frederic is trying to fit himself into the stereotype of "the nervous husband" so that his apprehension of death may seem nothing more than the typical cartoon-like gesture of the dishevelled, cigarette-smoking, anxious male. But as quickly as his mind touches upon generalizing stereotypes, it rejects them, for to Frederic all generalities are suspect. He has trained his mind to move from general statement to specific perception, from the word to the reality—and the reality of this situation is that no matter how typical indeed his fears may be, the possibility of Catherine's death in childbirth remains. Thus in these opening trial runs, Frederic cannot qualify his perception of the situation by clichés that cluster about "the anxious husband," just as earlier he could not conceive of war in clichés of sacrifice and glory.

The few medical clichés he calls to mind are destined to fail, since Frederic has already seen that medical jargon often conceals

sheer ignorance.[5] He tries to fit Catherine's pain into a larger
context of natural (and thus survivable) causes, but this approach
leads back to another fact of nature, the indisputable fact of death.
There remain the alternatives of reason and faith. What logical
reason is there for Catherine to die now? Having already dis-
counted the possibility of moral retribution for the sin of illicit
love, Frederic can find no other logic for her death. But he has
learned of the gratuitousness of death in war (Aymo's death, for
instance, and his own near execution), and he knows that death
strikes without discernible reason. Death is merely inevitable, not
rational. His final response is a simple declarative assertion of
faith: "She can't die." And this is the weakest position of all. So
Frederic's panic increases as he is flung back again and again to
the initial and still unanswered question, "But what if she should
die?"

The bewilderment and shock that Frederic feels are reflected
in the helpless repetition of this question and in the accelerated
pace with which it comes as his futile monologue draws to an end.
He has found no way out of the trap. But by refusing to capitulate
to the easy cliché and the sentimental illusion, he has maintained
intellectual and moral integrity. He has done this, however, at the
expense of all hope. At the conclusion of the monologue both he
and the reader have the clear foreknowledge of doom. The terrible anguish inextricably bound with this knowledge is created
through the "fourth dimensional" quality of Hemingway's writing,
its implicatory or suggestive power; it is the anguish inherent in
the frustrated and always circuitous movement of Frederic's
thoughts, the pathetic meagreness of his sentences, the bare banality of his phrases, as he races frantically back and forth, trapped
in a maze which has no exit. The alternative to escape, which
Frederic takes, is to acknowledge the truth of the situation, and
this acknowledgement is signified by the change of style, back to
his clipped and precise everyday speech.

Thus Hemingway's rejection of the loose and easy formulation
of the cliché, like Frederic's ultimate dismissal of it here, is in
effect a refusal to capitulate to any formulation at all. The search
for exactness of language becomes a moral act, implying an en-

---

[5] Compare the learned language of the doctors who cannot distinguish the
X-rays of the right leg from that of the left with the staccato, direct and
lively speech of Dr. Valentini. See pp. 99-101 and 103. As Robert Penn
Warren has noted, Dr. Valentini's "lingo" is like Rinaldi's in "its bantering,
ironical . . . tone that is the mark of the initiate." "Introduction" to *A
Farewell to Arms*, p. XXXI.

counter with reality; it is the search for a code not yet defined, hence not yet expressed, and certainly not yet made meaningless by unconsidered use. When, as in this passage in *A Farewell to Arms*, Hemingway uses the cliché he makes of it a moral standard by which character is tested and revealed.[6] And since character implies action, the cliché becomes also a device of plot to foreshadow and even to provide climactic resolution.[7] Thus style, character, and structure reinforce each other in the novel, and perception and language become truly reciprocal.

---

[6] I have elsewhere discussed how James T. Farrell has used the commonplace and banal language of the streets both to create and to make implicit comment on the sensibilities of his characters. See Blanche H. Gelfant, *The American City Novel* (Oklahoma: University of Oklahoma Press, 1954), pp. 209-217.

[7] The total implications of a language of truisms and clichés is currently being explored in "the theatre of the absurd." A work like Eugene Ionesco's *Rhinoceros*—which is so wildly different from *A Farewell to Arms*—pushes the language of clichés to an extreme to reveal not only the conformity of mind but, worse, the lack of contact with reality which underlies its use. Before the characters are transformed into rhinoceroses, they rationalize the value of such a metamorphosis by a series of clichés. Berenger, however, always pushes past the clichés to the fact—the very horrifying fact which the others always lose sight of—that a man is turning into an ugly and vicious animal. When at the end Berenger cries out that it is "too late" for him to make the transformation (although he might at last wish for it), I infer that this is perhaps because he has exhausted all the kinds of clichés which might have preceded, if indeed they did not cause, the change. He has seen the reality so persistently that words cannot now blind him to the ugly metamorphosis. When all the clichés have been suggested and have in turn been discarded, he must remain what he is, a man. See Eugene Ionesco, *Rhinoceros and Other Plays,* tr. by Derek Prouse (New York: Grove Press, Evergreen Edition, 1960).

John Graham

Ernest Hemingway: The Meaning of Style

Hemingway, in the opening pages of *Death in the Afternoon*, insists that he, his characters, and ultimately, his readers be aware of the active existence of persons, things, and actions. Too often, however, critics seem to accept this as meaning simply the accumulation of concrete details by a sensitive observer. Furthermore, the vitality of Hemingway's novels has been attributed to a number of factors ranging from his plots and characters to his simplicity of theme and control of language. These elements in their many aspects are, of course, contributory but are subordinate to a more constant cause: the active presentation of subject and object (observer and thing observed) and the continuous, intimate, and conscious relationship between subject and object. The characters' conscious reception of present fact (not judgment of or even response to fact) is so pervasive in Hemingway's novels that it appears to be a mode of thought for Hemingway, rather than a conscious artistic device. It is in this constant activity of sensory

Reprinted from *Modern Fiction Studies,* VI (1960-1961), 298-313 (revised 1970). Reprinted by permission of the author and *Modern Fiction Studies,* © 1969, by Purdue Research Foundation, Lafayette, Indiana.

perception of active objects, and, still more important, in the subjects' awareness of relationship to these objects that the vitality of the writing is found.

The total effect of activity in the novels is gained by a simplicity of plot, a directness of human relations, and a basic impermanence of situation. The major circumstances are keynoted by impermanency: the hero is in a foreign land or, in the case of Santiago of *The Old Man and the Sea*, a foreign element. No matter how familiar the protagonist may be with the place, he is not expected to settle there. The characters "use" countries, hotels, cafes, and houses, but there is never a real act of possession. The reader waits for the next move. The main plot is dominated by violence of war, combat and/or erratic movement from place to place; the characters reflect these highly unstable conditions by their attention on the immediate present and by their lack of demand on the future. They are active, direct and, one might argue, uncomplicated people with an almost fatalistic acceptance of life. Since they are so uncomplicated in their relations and attitudes, more of a burden falls on the "working out" of the action if the novel is not to die for lack of physical, emotional, or intellectual life.

These elements of circumstance, plot, and character achieve their effects of total vitality cumulatively rather than constantly. On the other hand, it is the continuous and aware relation of active subjects and objects that vivifies the novel at all times. By the nature of Hemingway's plot and characters, and his idea of conflict, the "movement" of this relation takes on added importance since, because of its pervasiveness, it sustains the vitality, giving more flexibility in the presentation of the other elements. Without going into extended detail, the plots of the novels are certainly no more vivid, often less so, than thousands of others. While the subject is often war or physical combat, which by their very nature are intensively active, such subjects, even when coupled with credible participants, do not guarantee life but simply physical exercise. The characters may fade in and out of the action, emotionally alert but divorced from the source of the emotion. Hemingway, with the possible exception of some ruminations of Robert Jordan in *For Whom the Bell Tolls*, does not permit his characters to retreat so far from the facts of their existence that the reader concentrates on the emotion rather than on the motivating force.

A second negative point concerning the importance of this sustaining element of relation with the active concrete is the lack of development of Hemingway's characters./In a surprisingly brief time, Hemingway establishes character; in the first few chapters the reader learns all he is to know about the central actors, and these actors are as knowing about each other as they are ever to be. The action and relations which follow serve only as illustrative incidents which fix more firmly what was openly presented and readily grasped many pages before. There is nothing new to learn; even with the various crises, the characters simply observe. While they seem to understand what they do and what goes on about them, they never seem to assimilate this knowledge and, if they react, they do not change as a result.[1] There would be a real danger of stagnation in the characters if they were not intimately aware of and actively connected with the active material world as well as the incidents in which they take part.

The final negative element that heightens the importance of movement is the lack of complexity in the conflicts presented in the novels. The simplicity, directness, and obviousness of the conflicts give the characters knowledge of the facts of their various situations. There is no challenge to the characters or the reader demanding extended mental activity, subtle or otherwise. The testimony of the participant's senses can be accepted as objective, if limited, fact. While such a simplicity is of value to a forward moving and well controlled narrative, it lessens the possibility of establishing tensions which will keep the novel alive and meaning-

---

[1] There is a prevailing doggedness, a form of passivity mixed with the major characters' acceptance of fact. They do not control their worlds but rather observe and react, accept and endure: Robert Jordan tenaciously follows orders (though admirably making the best of several bad bargains, i. e., the stolen exploder and his broken leg); Santiago does the usual and inevitable by trying to catch a fish and staying with one when it is hooked; Frederic Henry has only a negative solution by continuing "the retreat" from the war after he and Catherine reject the world which has interfered; Jake and Brett continue an impossible, aimless existence in spite of the knowledge of experience. (Brett is so unstable in her relations that her "action" of sending Pedro Romero away is as much a different way of expressing her inability for real intimacy as a revelation of any basic goodness.)

There is, however, a deepening of the relations of the hero as the novels progress: Frederic and Catherine, Robert and Maria, and Santiago and the fish. But these relations have only an immediate and temporary unity, one which has no existence outside the present situation. It is difficult to take the love affairs seriously for there is never a sense of permanency, future, which, I venture, is a necessary note of love. There is a romantic conjuring up of the flames of love for a physical and emotional security in the extremely unstable conditions in which the characters find themselves; there is an active attempt at getting what life may offer before life goes.

ful as it moves through its rises and falls. Vitality is preserved by the constant and conscious reception of more, though basically unvaried, information concerning the living world in which the characters operate.

The *constant* effect of vitality is gained by the rather obvious quick shifts (particularly within the unit of the paragraph) from one type of expression to another. The writing ranges freely and briefly through narration, description and exposition, monolog and dialog, and first, second and third persons.[2] Shifting points of view add a more organic variation to these essentially artificial devices. But the real force of life is conveyed by the *consciousness* of the relation between characters and an *active* material world. These relations may be physical, emotional or mental, active or static, and actual, potential, hypothetical, or desired.[3] They may be simple, one-directional relations, or become involved exchanges, expanding in both time and place.

This element of "movement" in Hemingway's novels can be observed even in his very brief and seemingly simple descriptions of people. In the description of the Russian, Karkov, there is a limited range of sensory perception, no present physical action on the part of the object, and a rather simple physical, emotional, and mental relation of subject to object:

> He had liked Karkov but not the place. Karkov was the most intelligent man he had ever met. Wearing black riding boots, gray breeches, and a gray tunic, with tiny hands and feet, puffily fragile of face and body, with a spitting way of talking through his bad teeth, he looked comic when Robert Jordan first saw him. But he had more brains and more inner dignity and outer insolence and humor than any man he had ever known.
>
> *For Whom the Bell Tolls*, p. 231.[4]

---

[2] This type of activity is in a sense outside the world of the novel because it relies on the activity of the reader who is making subtle adjustments to the different types of presentation. It is not an activity within the world of the novel but rather a part of the direct process of artistic communication.

[3] In connection with the preceding note, no relation is "static" as long as there is an observer to consider the relation, and Hemingway always has a direct observer. Even the "static physical," i. e., "the tree next to the house," demands an adjustment on the part of the observer. I do not wish to make too much of this point since it is not of immediate importance for the particular thesis at hand; it does, however, add one more constant to the present discussion.

[4] The editions cited in this study are *The Sun Also Rises* (New York, 1957), *A Farewell to Arms* (New York, 1929), *For Whom the Bell Tolls* (New York, 1940), *Across the River and into the Trees* (New York, 1950), and *The Old Man and the Sea* (New York, 1955), all issued by Scribner.

Even in such a seemingly ordinary paragraph there is much conscious relation and active detail. The opening statement of Robert
Jordan's reminiscence first connects him with Karkov and indi-
cates generally the atmosphere of the relations; this is emphasized
by the concluding phrase *but not the place*, which also forces the
question "why?", then "why not?" to become prominent. This
question leads to the second which explains the first and implies,
by *most intelligent* and *ever*, an act of evaluation and the passage
of time. *Had . . . met* is the direct physical and social act which
leads to the description of Karkov. The description is brief, rather
disorderly, but ranging progressively in detail from clothing to
physique to typical action. The inanimate articles are given a type
of life by their relation to Karkov, by the participles *wearing* and
riding and by the reader's action of forming a uniform from the
separate pieces of clothing. The mannerism, *a spitting way of talking through his bad teeth*, presents two actions with a relation
between each other and a further relation to an audience, specific
and general. The concluding detail, *his bad teeth*, is connected
intimately with the verb *talking* by the preposition *through* which
in itself is an "active" preposition denoting passage from one place
to another. The independent clause presents an active judgment,
looked comic, the temporal clause reveals an implied continuation
of physical relation by the adverb *first*. *First* also anticipates the
later change of Jordan's conclusion which is revealed in the next
sentence, a concluding statement of Robert Jordan's opinion of
Karkov. This statement has the implied comparison with other
men, then a connection between Jordan and Karkov in *had ever
known*, and a shift from *inner* to *outer* man.

Robert Jordan, the subject, has a definite activity here of both
the senses and the judgment; his relation to the object, Karkov,
is not only logically set forth but is explicitly reiterated. Action
for Karkov is restricted and potential, but he is the cause of the
activities of Jordan. The interplay of the content and the implications of the perception present the basis for the mental activity
of the reader.

Other descriptions are more complex, expanding in time and in
place and presenting reciprocal relationships. While Karkov may
be considered "potential activity," Santiago is the result of the
passage of time and action:

> The old man was thin and gaunt with deep wrinkles in the back
> of his neck. The brown blotches of the benevolent skin cancer

the sun brings from its reflection on the tropic sea were on his cheeks. The blotches ran well down the sides of his face and his hands had the deep-creased scars from handling heavy fish on the cords. But none of these scars were fresh. They were as old as erosions in a fishless desert.

The Old Man and the Sea, pp. 9-10.

The activity and unity here is one of cause and effect; the continuous action of nature and of past experience on the old man has produced the present figure. Although the old man is "doing" nothing, the involvement of the relationships (indicated by the blotches and scars, the results, which exist in the present) gives a history of past action and forces the reader to shift from one point to another for his perspective and evaluation of the scene and condition.

Both Karkov and Santiago are presented with a sufficient amount of concrete detail for the reader to gain a direct and concrete picture of the characters. The approach to Brett Ashley is, however, quite different. In the entire novel, the only static details we are given about Brett are that her hair is short and her figure slender. She is attractive. There is no attempt at *ut pictura poesis,* no set piece as in Scott or Balzac. Hemingway gives Brett "body" by suggesting to the reader a type: he reveals her in settings, attitudes, and actions that bring out a compulsive, jaded, unconventional animalism, and the reader may choose, from imagination or experience, the physical embodiment for these qualities. A pertinent quotation may be drawn from Jake's observation in a Paris scene: Jake and Bill have come up to a bar; Mike strides forward and greets Jake cheerily; the two talk socially:

> Bill had gone into the bar. He was standing talking with Brett, who was sitting on a high stool, her legs crossed. She had no stockings on.
>
> *The Sun Also Rises,* p. 78.

The point of concentration which has existed for the long evening has been broken; the reader no longer sees the relaxed Bill-Jake combination but an unsettled one of Mike-Jake. The reader's line of observation moves from Jake, one half of the original point of concentration, to Bill, the other half, who is the immediate object of Jake's vision. Bill Gorton has not waited for an introduction to Mike (who certainly makes himself conspicuous) but goes straightway to Brett, Brett who sits reigning insolently on a high bar stool.

This shift uses the person we are with, Bill, to draw us closer to Brett, who has just come into range.

The shift demanded is not only a physical one but an emotional one involving change of tone. Jake, surrounded by the alcoholic garrulity of Mike, is in sharp contrast with the intimacy of the conversation at the bar. The present activity of Brett and Bill *talking*, the past activity of shifting up onto the *high* stool and of crossing her legs and the partially incompleted past action of dressing (*no stockings*), fills the paragraph with an undercurrent of physical activity contributing to the scene's vitality. A still further note of vitality lies in Jake's either intellectual or emotional disapproval of this scene, a scene which expands, reaching through the novel and presenting Brett for what she is: attractive, alcoholic, unconventional, loose and inclined to justify her activities. The reader is given the woman in her particular active relation to particular friends, places, and actions; the character and life are there, although Brett herself is not defined overtly or given a set, static description.

Within the limits of the paragraph, the unit under discussion, vitality might be achieved most easily and effectively in a scene emphasizing the relationships of human beings who were reacting to each other on a number of levels and with varying intensity. While this is true and important for complexity, Hemingway often gains surprisingly active effects with the simple relations of a human subject and an inanimate object to preserve a sense of continuous vitality and to instill an awareness of an immediate and direct contact with the physical world. In an act of seemingly casual observation, Robert Jordan's eyes shift from one point to another as he looks at the snow stretched out before the machine gun:

> The sun was bright on the snow and it was melting fast. He could see it hollowing away from the tree trunks and just ahead of the gun, before his eyes, the snow surface was damp and lacily fragile as the heat of the sun melted the top and the warmth of the earth breathed warmly up at the snow that lay upon it.
>
> *For Whom the Bell Tolls,* p. 282.

Not only is Robert Jordan aware of the existence of the snow, but the snow is in active relation to the sun, the trees, and the earth, changing before the man's gaze. The sun and the earth act on the snow, transforming it; the snow acts in relation to the trees, withdrawing from them; and the snow surface has a static relation (its position) ahead of the gun, before his eyes. The interconnected activity of the inanimate has its own life, independent of the observer yet in relation to him.

While Robert Jordan is rather passively conscious of the active snow object above, he is physically and emotionally very actively conscious of the view and of his relation to it as he lies above the bridge waiting for dawn and the attack.

> Robert Jordan lay behind the trunk of a pine tree on the slope of the hill above the road and the bridge and watched it become daylight. He loved this hour of the day always and now he watched it; feeling it gray within him, as though he were a part of the slow lightening that comes before the rising of the sun; when solid things darken and space lightens and the lights that have shown in the night go yellow and fade as the day comes. The pine trunks below him were hard and clear now, their trunks solid and brown and the road was shiny with a wisp of mist over it. The dew had wet him and the forest floor was soft and he felt the give of the brown, dropped pine needles under his elbows. Below he saw, through the light mist that rose from the stream bed, the steel of the bridge, straight and rigid across the gap, with the wooden sentry boxes at each end. But as he looked the structure of the bridge was still spidery and fine in the mist that hung over the stream.
>
> *For Whom the Bell Tolls*, p. 431.[5]

The activity and relations here are many and varied, but the scene is dominated by Jordan's observation of and identification with the coming light and the hanging mist. In this fluid context, he shifts his gaze from detail to detail and watches as the objects grow clearer. He is acted upon (wet by the dew), reacts (feels) to a movement (the give of the forest floor). The vividness of the activity of light and of the connection of detail with detail in a static physical relation is ultimately dependent on the unity and vitality of Jordan's awareness of his sense perceptions.

To emphasize this intimate connection between subject and object, and their mutual relation to activity, Hemingway is fond of presenting a picture of the countryside as seen by a moving observer. Perhaps "picture" is inexact for it is rather an impression

---

[5] The tactile element in this paragraph is balanced by the visual. For paragraphs of exclusively tactile awareness, see those presenting Jordan checking his packs (p. 48) and readying his submachine gun (p. 431).

which reveals the movements of the observer on an equal scale with the general nature of the landscapes. The activity of the single observer's continually changing perspectives and objects is transferred to the rather disconnected details and unifies and vivifies them. A simple example of this approach may be drawn from the trip that Jake and Bill take from Paris to Bayonne:

> We ate the sandwiches and drank the Chablis and watched the country out of the window. The grain was just beginning to ripen and the fields were full of poppies. The pastureland was green, and there were fine trees, and sometimes big rivers and chateaux off in the trees.
>
> *The Sun Also Rises*, p. 87.[6]

Here the vitality of the rich growth of the expanding vista is closely connected to the vitality of the aware and pleased observer, and the gain is mutually reinforcing.

An additional virtue of these travel episodes is that the action has a consciously sought goal of a destination which aids in the movement; "the bridge" in *For Whom the Bell Tolls* serves in a similar capacity, generating an almost compulsive drive toward a conclusion. The sense of conscious purpose in the activity of a character can increase the intensity of a scene, putting a particular demand on the person as, for example, during the retreat from Caporetto: Hemingway is not simply "picturing" or establishing an external world in which his characters will operate in some possible future. The character observes and records that external world because he *must* understand it.

> Crossing the field, I did not know but that someone would fire on us from the trees near the farmhouse or from the farmhouse itself. I walked toward it, seeing it very clearly. The balcony of the second floor merged into the barn and there was hay coming out between the columns. The courtyard was of stone blocks and all the trees were dripping with the rain. There was a big empty two-wheeled cart, the shafts tipped high up in the rain. I came to the courtyard, crossed it, and stood under the shelter of the balcony. The door of the house was open and I went in. Bonello and

---

[6] Compare Jake and Bill on the bus ride to Burguette (p. 108) and during their walk through the beech wood (p. 120) in *The Sun Also Rises* as well as Colonel Cantwell in *Across the River and into the Trees* (p. 14).

Piani came in after me. It was dark inside. I went back to the
kitchen. There were ashes of a fire on the big open hearth. The
pots hung over the ashes, but they were empty.

A Farewell to Arms, pp. 229-230.

Here the goal of the subject is not simply one of perception or
destination but of specific and necessary information. As he crosses
the field to reach the farmhouse, Frederic describes the place in
active terms but the description is, in a sense, accidental to his act
of peering for an enemy. This farmhouse has a vital and direct
significance to Frederic; it is not presented simply as a concrete
detail in a landscape. The "purposeful observation" is the usual
method employed for the apparently "incidental" presentation of
concrete surroundings. Sometimes the description will have an
immediate and specific significance; at others a very general one.
This utilitarian aspect of observation is one of the strongest links
between the characters and their world.

An interesting aspect of this purposeful relation between the
observer and the world is the semi-professional view that the
characters often take of their world as if they were evaluating it
for an immediate or future specific use. The major characters often
reveal a handbook view of an object, a view conditioned by their
function as professional observers. Santiago looks at sky, water,
and light for indications of future weather and fishing conditions.
Frederic and Robert, as soldiers, consider roads, bridges, and terrain in terms of men, movement, and equipment, though Frederic
Henry does so with a dull and jaded eye while Robert Jordan is
always interested and often pleased; finally, Jake, the newspaper
man, views spectacles in the colorful manner that might be expected of a journalist and sojourner. These special variations of
purposeful observation are the results of two basic conditions of
the Hemingway protagonists that elicit the consciousness of particular or professional knowledge. The hero is often a foreigner;
even though he may know the language fluently, he is in some way
an outsider, not really in the stream of tradition or daily life. As a
result he must learn rather consciously as much as possible about
the alien world if he is to deal with it; terrain and customs must
be assimilated. Furthermore, while the hero's senses are alerted in
his learning process, he, as a "professional," has something to teach
the other characters, whether it be bull fighting, warfare, fishing,
or eating and drinking. The hero as either student or teacher needs

to be aware of the world around him—persons as well as places and things—if he is to survive as a personality and, often, as a physical entity.[7]

The final example of a presentation of the inanimate is an extremely carefully worked out picture of the bull corral in *The Sun Also Rises*. An orderly inter-weaving of concrete detail and of the crowd's restrained activity carries the observing party from the ticket gate to the top of the wall; the simple, direct narration of activity and the orderly expanding description are such that neither could have existence (to say nothing of meaning and vitality) without the order. The eye does not stop at the top of the wall; the area is opened and expands up and out to the horizon, gathering more details and more aspects of life, in particular, people who are in turn focusing their gaze toward the center of the scene.

"Look up there," I said.
Beyond the river rose the plateau of the town. All along the old walls and ramparts people were standing. The three lines of forti-

---

[7] These teacher-learner relations function not only within the world of the novel but extend to the reader. The two premises—hero as foreigner and hero as professional—encourage the reader's identification with the protagonist as learner as well as submission to his (teacher's) knowledge and experience. The reader is inclined to identify himself with the hero-foreigner since the reader himself is a stranger who accepts and welcomes information given by the author (either directly or indirectly), the presentation of which he would find obtrusive under other circumstances. This attitude is not limited to acceptance of fact, but after conditioning the reader to accept him as guide to the facts of the situation, the author is in a more authoritative position in any statement he makes or impression he conveys. In some particular sphere, however, the author is often knowledgeable. The "teaching" aspect in Hemingway's novels may be divided into three basic facets: 1. Characters teach characters: Jake teaches Brett about bullfighting (Ch. XIII), peasants teach Bill how to drink wine from a skin (Ch. XI), Karkov teaches Robert Jordan his politics (Ch. XVIII), Robert Jordan teaches gun placement and observation (Ch. XXII & XLIII); 2. Hemingway teaches reader directly: Afición, *The Sun Also Rises* (Ch. XIII), France and tipping, *The Sun Also Rises* (Ch. XIX), and fishing methods, *The Old Man and the Sea*; 3. Hemingway teaches reader indirectly: Jake prepares trout (Ch. XII), Santiago prepares fish (p. 47), and Jordan makes a bough bed (Ch. XX) and loads a gun (Ch. XLI). James B. Colvert, in "Hemingway's Morality in Action," *AL*, XXVII (1955), 384, quite rightly argues that Hemingway's women are all "students" of the heroes, and references to Hemingway's concern for professional knowledge and attitude may be found in Joseph Beaver, "Technique in Hemingway," *College English*, XIV (1952-53), 325-328 and Charles A. Fenton, "No Money for the Kingbird: Hemingway's Prizefight Stories," *American Quarterly*, IV (1952), 839-850. I believe the major problem in *Across the River and into the Trees* is that the teacher-learner attitude is grossly out of control.

fications made three black lines of people. Above the walls there
were heads in the windows of the houses. At the far end of the
plateau boys had climbed into the trees.

The Sun Also Rises, p. 138.[8]

Just as the composition of a painting directs the viewer's eye to
rest or to follow a certain direction, so this place, the first-person
narrator, and Hemingway's description urge the reader to move
from one concentric ring to another. It is as if the viewer were a
sentient stone sending out ripples in a pool, aware of the expanding circles and the movement of points (i.e., people) on them.

Until this stage the examples considered have been of relationships of persons, places, and things. These relationships have been
active, significant, and recognized by the observer. The emphasis
has been on the concrete fact rather than on incident. The following examples have been chosen as examples of action but they are
more than that alone; the combination of narration and description does not make the distinction of "descriptive unit" or "narrative unit" simple and clearcut. But then this is just one more of
the devices for integrating all aspects of the life presented in the
novels.

Within the context of the regular plot of the novel, there will
be many incidents of subordinate actions contributing toward the
whole. To drive the point further, parts of incidents are again
subordinate actions contributing to their particular whole. Obviously this can be pushed back to the sentence or phrase or even
word, each element being filled with actual or potential movement.
The extent to which the writer "packs" his action scenes is, of
course, dependent on the precise effect he wishes to achieve, but
Hemingway's tendency is toward gaining as much internal action
as possible and relating it closely to the characters.

The simplest form of action is the rather automatic performance
of commonplace deeds. The flat economy of this narrative or type
can achieve a variety of effects, especially when used for contrast,
but more significantly the act described is the narrator's attempt
to get out of his unrecognizable emotions, to establish contact
with the non-self. The drained Jake retreats to San Sebastian
after the fiesta:

I unpacked my bags and stacked my books on the table beside
the head of my bed, put out my shaving things, hung up some

---

[8] Compare the view from the bus in *The Sun Also Rises* (p. 108).

clothes in the big armoire, and made up a bundle for the laundry. Then I took a shower in the bathroom and went down to lunch. Spain had not changed to summertime, so I was early. I set my watch again. I had recovered an hour by coming to San Sebastian.
The Sun Also Rises, p. 234.

Jake must "establish" himself in San Sebastian, must be consciously aware of his relation to a world just as he was aware when he and Bill walked through Paris or fished in a stream. It is a part of the self-centeredness of the Hemingway protagonist who must relate all things to himself if either self or things is to have meaning. He must make a world of conscious relation. Slowly the detachment is overcome, slowly a richness of consciousness emerges, and Jake can again enjoy as well as perceive.

I walked around the harbor under the trees to the casino, and then up one of the cool streets to the Cafe Marinas. There was an orchestra playing inside the café and I sat out on the terrace and enjoyed the fresh coolness in the hot day, and had a glass of lemon-juice and shaved ice and then a long whiskey and soda. I sat in front of the Marinas for a long time and read, and watched the people, and listened to the music.
The Sun Also Rises, p. 235.

The world and Jake's orderly relation to it have been reasserted. The impersonality is gone, and Jake can contact only the life he wishes and come alive. The actions of the subject, the passage of time, the sights, sounds, tastes, and the transition from the heat of the day to the cool of the evening all fill this paragraph with a leisurely movement of quiet consciousness.

To the relaxed action of this scene an interesting contrast is the animal vigor and pleasure of Rafael, the gypsy, as he walks toward Robert Jordan, who has just killed a cavalry man and is setting up a machine gun in anticipation of discovery and attack:

Just then, while he was watching all of the country that was visible, he saw the gypsy coming through the rocks to the left. He was walking with a loose, high-hipped, sloppy swing, his carbine was slung on his back, his brown face was grinning and he carried two big hares, one in each hand. He carried them by the legs, heads swinging.
For Whom the Bell Tolls, p. 474.

Not only is his walk animated but his whole body is working: arms, hands, face. Even the dead rabbits are a part of the action as they swing in the gypsy's grasp.

As satisfying as these presentations may be in their movement, restraint, and solidity, one turns with interest to the presentation of violent actions such as that of the bull's entrance in *The Sun Also Rises*:

> I leaned way over the wall and tried to see into the cage. It was dark. Some one rapped on the cage with an iron bar. Inside something seemed to explode. The bull, striking into the wood from side to side with his horns, made a great noise. Then I saw a dark muzzle and the shadow of horns, and then, with a clattering on the wood on the hollow box, the bull charged and came out into the corral, skidding with his forefeet in the straw as he stopped, his head up, the great hump of muscle on his neck swollen tight, his body muscles quivering as he looked up at the crowd on the stone walls. The two steers backed away against the wall, their heads sunken, their eyes watching the bull.
>
> *The Sun Also Rises,* pp. 138-139.[9]

The activity here is literally explosive as the bull bursts from the dark of the cage into the sunlight of the corral. Jake's anticipatory action establishes him as a concerned part of the scene; the heralding noises prepare for the entrance; then the charging, quivering bull dominates the picture. The bull defies the crowd; the steers wait with frightened resignation. Except for the crowd itself, all relationships here are active and intense and anticipate future action.

The simplicity and directness of the lines of actions in the examples already cited give an immediacy of impact and a quick-paced reception of active fact. More complex devices of presentation vary and control this communication. One technique employed is the revelation by grammatical structure of separate but concurrent actions that become mutually involved. United by no logical relation or by cause and effect, the actions draw into closer relation characters or things which reveal or clarify each other. One obvious use of this device may be observed in *For Whom the Bell Tolls*:

---

[9] Compare the description of the fish breaking water in *The Old Man and the Sea* (p. 69) and *Islands in the Stream* (New York, 1970), p. 121.

Robert Jordan unrolled the bundle of clothing that made his pillow and pulled on his shirt. It was over his head and he was pulling it down when he heard the next planes coming and he pulled his trousers on over the robe and lay still as three more of the Heinkel bimotor bombers came over. Before they were gone over the shoulder of the mountain, he had buckled on his pistol, rolled the robe and placed it against the rocks, and sat now, close against the rocks, tying his ropesoled shoes, when the approaching droning turned to a greater clattering roar than ever before and nine more Heinkel light bombers came in echelons; hammering the sky apart as they went over.

For Whom the Bell Tolls, p. 75.[10]

The two actions are channeled grammatically—Robert Jordan's dressing in the independent clauses, the planes' flight in the temporal ones. The independent clauses present a base of commonplace activity and flat rhythm from which operates the harshly poetic flight and the climactic rhythm of the dependent clauses. It is through the earthborn, the personal, the individual of the guerrilla that we approach the diabolic symbol of distant, impersonal mechanization.

Another method of involving forward pace while keeping the action immediately alive is to shift from one object to another with a real or implied shift of subject:

The count was looking at Brett across the table under the gaslight. She was smoking a cigarette and flicking the ashes on the rug. She saw me notice it. "I say, Jake, I don't want to ruin your rugs. Can't you give a chap an ashtray?"

The Sun Also Rises, p. 57.

Jake, the subject, looked at the count who was watching Brett; the subject momentarily and implicitly shifts from Jake to the count, the object from the count to Brett. Then Brett's action of flicking the ashes occurred; "When she saw me notice it," the subject becomes Brett, the object, Jake, and then is immediately reversed. Brett requested an ashtray in a vaguely guilty manner. The shifting of subject and object, and the limited action of the scene have combined to form a vital whole. The intimate relation of Jake and Brett, her attractiveness to other men and her awareness of that

---

[10] Compare Jordan's concurrent awareness of his watch (time) and Maria in *For Whom the Bell Tolls* (p. 378).

attraction, her carelessness and Jake's control over that carelessness, are all revealed in the conscious observations in these few
lines. The significant interplay is alive and active within itself
without having any direct role in a specific incident in the usual
meaning of the term.

In the preceding scene, the people are conscious of themselves
and of each other. A different type of consciousness, more intro-
spective and articulated, is presented by Frederic Henry as he
floats down the icy river, clinging to a heavy timber. Not only is
he uncomfortably aware of the present and very much involved
in it, but his thoughts range back and forth in time and place.

> You do not know how long you are in a river when the current
> moves swiftly. It seems a long time and it may be very short. The
> water was cold and in flood and many things passed that had
> been floated off the banks when the river rose. I was lucky to have
> a heavy timber to hold on to, and I lay in the icy water with my
> chin on the wood, holding as easily as I could with both hands.
> I was afraid of cramps and I hoped we would move toward the
> shore. We went down the river in a long curve. It was beginning
> to be light enough so I could see the bushes along the shore-
> line. There was a brush island ahead and the current moved
> toward the shore. I wondered if I should take off my boots and
> clothes and try to swim ashore, but I decided not to. I had never
> thought of anything but that I would reach the shore some way,
> and I would be in a bad position if I landed barefoot. I had to
> get to Mestre some way.
>
> *A Farewell to Arms*, p. 242.

The activity of the subject, both mental and physical, is continuous as is the contact with the reader. The lieutenant explains to
the reader the sensation in the river and the problem of judgment,
considers cause and effect, admits good fortune, fears, accounts,
speculates, judges, anticipates, and then doggedly fixes his mind
on getting "to Mestre some way." His is an observation and con-
sideration of both the facts and the possibilities of the situation
in which he finds himself.

This intense sense of involvement with the present action, as is
quietly revealed in the foregoing quotation, is nowhere more
brilliantly dramatized than in the opening scene of Chapter XXI,
pp. 265ff. from *For Whom the Bell Tolls*, a section too long for
inclusion here. In this incident, the vivid description and rushing
action fuse into a whole in which the characters act, react, and are

acted upon. After opening rather "idyllically" in the quiet peace of
the morning, the sound of hoofbeats comes to Robert Jordan,
anticipating the entrance of the young cavalryman. The dynamiter
is caught up immediately in a three-way relation: he warns Maria,
readies himself, and watches for a horseman. The rider appears
and the pistol roars; the man is killed and the camp aroused to
frantic activity.

The section is vivid, economical, and controlled. To consider just
a part of it:

> He reached his hand down toward the scabbard and as he
> swung low, turning and jerking at the scabbard, Robert Jordan
> saw the scarlet of the formalized device he wore on the left breast
> of his khaki blanket cape.
> Aiming at the center of his chest, a little lower than the device,
> Robert Jordan fired.
> The pistol roared in the snowy woods.
>
> *For Whom the Bell Tolls*, p. 265.

The brilliance of the movement, detail, and sound merge to give
a piercing sensory impression. The simplicity of *the pistol roared
in the snowy woods* has been prepared for in every respect: the
quiet country setting with the snow melting and falling is shattered
by the harsh shot ringing from the heavy automatic pistol held in
both hands. The idyllic is broken by the ugly; we knew both
existed but their juxtaposition gives us the drama. Both of these
elements are picked up again as the scene is worked out; the
cavalryman is dragged through the snow, the horse tracks are a
matter of concern, and Robert Jordan nervously comments on the
pistol and lanyard, as he reloads. The entire section is the perfect
example of the union of vital parts in a living frame to produce a
dramatic and significant reality. All facets previously discussed
have been integrated in this passage.

There are three factors which have been examined in this study:
one, the object which is under observation; two, the subject, who,
in one way or another, does the observing; and three, the nature
of the relation between subject and object. Because of the usual
integration of these three aspects, it has been unnecessary and
impossible to prescind too sharply from any two. The conclusions
reached from these discussions are briefly: the activity of the object and subject may be either physical, emotional, or mental.
These activities may be presented as actual, potential, hypothetical, desired, past, or implied. The relation of the subject and

object is most often one of conscious or effective recognition by one or more of the senses; the subject often seeks to observe the object for a specific, sometimes necessary, purpose. (The reader, acting as external subject, must make subtle adjustments to varying types of expression.) The sense of immediacy in Hemingway's novels is gained not by the reproduction of the object for itself or even in the perception of the object by the subject so much as by the subject's awareness of his act of perception and the activity of the object perceived.

These are pedestrian facts by way of conclusion. The actual use of this view gives a concretely interrelated world to which the characters continually testify as present *now* and accounts for Hemingway's particular achievement in such vivid scenes as the fishing trip in *The Sun Also Rises*. Depending little on the cataloging of static details in the manner of Zola and Norris, Hemingway constructs the connection of character and action which always enlivens and solidifies the characters and humanizes scenes and actions. Before, and below the level of, the formation of the Hemingway "code"—his ideal of actions, courage, endurance, and technical competency—lies the involvement with and awareness of the material and interrelated world and of the characters' recognition of that active world. This constant movement gives the novels their vitality.[11]

[11] Since this study was first issued almost ten years ago, I should direct the reader to Earl Rovit's *Ernest Hemingway* (New York, 1963), especially chapters II and VI which contain a number of fruitful applications and developments of some points expressed in my article. See also C. P. Heaton, "Style in *The Old Man and the Sea*," Style, IV (1970), 11-27.